Above the Clouds

Managing Risk in the World of Cloud Computing

Above the Clouds

Managing Risk in the World of Cloud Computing

KEVIN T. MCDONALD

IT Governance Publishing

Every possible effort has been made to ensure that the information contained in this book is accurate at the time of going to press, and the publishers and the author cannot accept responsibility for any errors or omissions, however caused. No responsibility for loss or damage occasioned to any person acting, or refraining from action, as a result of the material in this publication can be accepted by the publisher or the author.

Apart from any fair dealing for the purposes of research or private study, or criticism or review, as permitted under the Copyright, Designs and Patents Act 1988, this publication may only be reproduced, stored or transmitted, in any form, or by any means, with the prior permission in writing of the publisher or, in the case of reprographic reproduction, in accordance with the terms of licences issued by the Copyright Licensing Agency. Enquiries concerning reproduction outside those terms should be sent to the publishers at the following address:

IT Governance Publishing
IT Governance Limited
Unit 3, Clive Court
Bartholomew's Walk
Cambridgeshire Business Park
Ely
Cambridgeshire
CB7 4EH
United Kingdom

www.itgovernance.co.uk

First published in the United Kingdom in 2010
by IT Governance Publishing.

ISBN 978-1-84928-031-0

PREFACE

What is Cloud Computing?

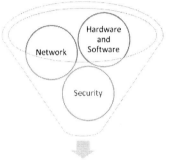

Utility Computing

Figure 1: Cloud Computing paradigm

Let's start with a definition. In the simplest, cocktail-hour terms, Cloud Computing is managed, shared applications, development platforms or computing infrastructure accessible via a network such as the Internet.

If you have a Gmail or Yahoo® account, you are already using Cloud Computing. You really don't know where your e-mail and contacts are stored; you access your account via the Internet or on a smartphone with the same simplicity and belief with which you turn on a light switch.

Cloud Computing provides options like bandwidth and computing power on demand, with elastic abilities usually paid for as a metered service or chargeback. Your organization may already provide a service like that without calling it Cloud Computing.

Shared service model

The concept of shifting computing to a shared service provider is not new. What may be new is that the cost of Cloud Computing is falling so dramatically that considering outsourcing to the Cloud is no longer rare, and it is now accessible enough that any individual or organization can use it to their advantage.

Computing as a commodity service

The commoditization of software and hardware that will appear and run the same whether they are set up by in-house IT staff or somewhere out in the ether are also factors. If the result is the same, the risks are more or less equivalent and the cost per transaction is dropping much faster outside the organization than when being performed in-house, the question that should be asked is when, not why.

Simplicity *versus* complexity

Another driver is simplicity. Information technology grows more complex over time. This complexity comes at a high price. The more complex the environment, the more prone it is to failure. The more prone to failure, the more difficult and intransigent systems are to change.

As our information systems have grown more complex, the data center bureaucracy has become more entrenched. We also may have lost sight of what they were supposed to accomplish for us in the first place. As a result, the percentage of work in IT that is dedicated to simply keeping the lights on and the machines humming has grown year to year. Meanwhile the actual amount of usable information from our "information" systems has not kept pace.

Data center efficiency

Studies indicate that a data center only uses, on average, 10 to 15% of its available capacity. By using a shared-resource Cloud model, we can regain much of this idle capacity and lower operating costs to as much as 80% below dedicated computing models. This explains in part why so much buzz surrounds Cloud Computing. The ability to rent IT services *versus* buy them, run existing IT resources more efficiently and throw the resources back when they aren't needed is very attractive in an era of increasingly tighter budgets.

The way ahead

If discussing factors such as reduced cost, commodity services, simplicity and efficiency, leaves you with that gnawing feeling that your organization is missing something in this complex IT arena, do not despair. It is likely your competitors are not performing any better.

There will always likely be a gap between where you are and where you could be on the scale of operational efficiency. Clues to the existence and magnitude of the gap lie in the geometric growth of things like chillers and pipes, routers and firewalls with no corresponding improvement in performance.

What if we could just jettison all of the details and get back to concentrating on functions and capabilities? Back to the days when the high priests of IT in white lab coats ushered in solutions instead of problems and fear.

Cloud Computing creates the impression that we no longer need to have a handle on the details, just as we don't need to understand electricity to use it. Cloud Computing holds the promise that we just need to step up, flip the switch and let data flow from the Cloud. Can we trade the data center utility for a utility bill?

That is, of course, the promise. The question is how do we get there?

ABOUT THE AUTHOR

Kevin T. McDonald is a senior information technology analyst and Cloud strategist for ICF International, Inc., a global consultancy based in Washington, DC. Mr McDonald is an imaginative IT security and project leader with over 25 years of industry and government experience. He specializes in infrastructure protection, cybersecurity, and business continuity planning for government and commercial clients and has published and spoken in a variety of venues.

He is a member of the Tech America Cloud Computing Committee, the IAC-ACT Cross-SIG Cloud Computing in Government committee and the Cloud Security Alliance.

He holds a Bachelor of Science in business administration (BSBA) Information Systems and Quantitative Analysis program from the University of Arkansas and is currently pursing graduate studies at Georgetown University in Washington, DC.

Mr McDonald holds certifications from the International Information Systems Security Certification Consortium, Inc. ((ISC)²®) as a certified information systems security professional (CISSP), from the Systems Audit and Control Association (ISACA) as a certified information systems auditor (CISA), from the Project Management Institute as a project management professional (PMP) and is a certified business continuity professional (CBCP) from the Disaster Recovery Institute International. He lives in Falls Church, Virginia, with his wife Melanie.

ACKNOWLEDGEMENTS

There is not enough space to thank all who have contributed to this work. Great thanks to Angela at IT Governance for her unflagging cheer and patience and to Chris Peters and Andy Robison at ICF for their early and continuous support. To my father Paul, for sharing his love of ideas, and my mother Kathleen, for sharing the wisdom to bring them into reality. And finally, for Melanie, my wife, my friend and my muse; nothing happened until she happened. Falls Church, 2009.

CONTENTS

Contents

Contents

Contents

Contents

INTRODUCTION

When discussing Cloud Computing, it is helpful to have a lexicon of common terms handy. Additional resources and expanded definitions are available on the National Institute of Standards and Technology website that have contributed greatly to the discussion of Cloud Computing.

http://csrc.nist.gov/groups/SNS/cloud-computing/

Cloud Computing provides widely accessible, on-demand, elastic computing power. These services are metered and charged back based on usage.

The capital investment in the data center is assumed by the Cloud provider and operation costs are passed on to the Cloud data center users. This shifting from a capital-intensive model to an operating-expense model shifts the material risk somewhat from the service user to the service provider.

The service provider is stuck with the equipment and data center assets. The service user is usually on a month-to-month or an annual contract to the service provider. Cancel the contract and the service user is not obligated for the disposal of the equipment.

Contrast that with a data center owner/operator. The hardware and software expense must be sufficient to provide services for the high-water mark of demand. If demand falls, they are still on the hook for the equipment.

Virtualization

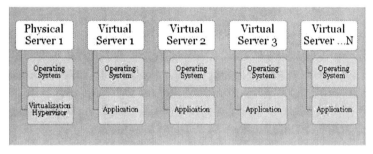

Figure 2: Virtualization

One of the features of Cloud Computing is that the computing power and storage capacity are elastic and can grow or shrink based upon your needs. One way to imagine how this is done is to visualize a magic refrigerator. Each time you open the door, only the food that you like appears. When another person opens the door, they have an entirely different experience. Physically, from the outside, it looks like the same refrigerator, but when you open it, *voilà* (there you are), a unique experience.

Virtual computing works much the same way for Cloud Computing. When your computer connects to the Cloud, each web address that you enter brings up a unique web page with unique characteristics. If the web server is running a virtual environment, the same hardware can host many different websites, all different, all with a unique address.

Virtualization is what gets this done

Virtualization is a process of creating a copy in software of a physical machine. The user of the machine appears to have the full resources of the machine at their disposal. In reality, the machine is only devoting a portion of its overall capacity to supporting this one user. The remaining capacity is divided among many other users, all running their own copy of the machine. From the perspective of the computer user, one is not aware of any other job running on the same machine. Thus the term virtual machine was coined.

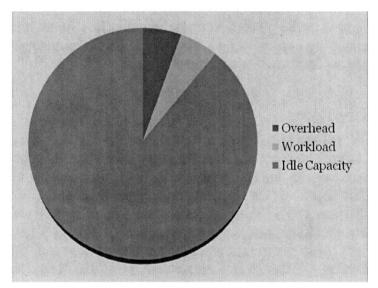

Figure 3: Average server utilization

Time slice

This concept is very closely related to the time-sharing concept coined in the 60s. Each computer's time is divided into slices. Each processing slice or cycle is run to some logical conclusion; the state of the machine is saved onto disk or into memory; the next job is pulled in, it is processed a bit more, then saved and so on. Eventually, the job receives enough cycles or time slices to complete processing.

Studies have shown that the average data center only utilizes 10 to 25% of its processing power. By using virtualization to share computers between millions of users, a Cloud model can increase utilization and provide computing power at a lower cost.

Gaining an 80 to 90% increase in utilization of existing servers by consolidating users into a shared environment reduces the overall cost of computing.

Hypervisor

The software that runs all of the copies of the virtual machines and makes sure that they don't use the same resources simultaneously is called a hypervisor. Among the more popular of the virtual machine hypervisors are EMC's VMware, Citrix®'s Xenworks and the Linux Open Source product Kernel-based Virtual Machine (KVM). All have their particular adherents. But for the purposes of this discussion, the most important point is that the virtualization software is what is used to manage the workload on a particular machine.

Public, private, community and hybrid Clouds

The delivery model is usually broken up into four modes: public, private, community and hybrid delivery of Cloud services.

Public Clouds

Public Clouds generally feature clients from more than one organization sharing the same infrastructure. This is also known as multi-tenancy.

In a public Cloud, a third-party service provider sells shared computing resources. Since the provider is in business to make a profit, there is a physical limit to the amount of computing capacity available at any one time and thus they will only agree to minimum service levels unless the organization is willing to pay a premium. This is contractually agreed upon ahead of time in a service level agreement.

The agreement will not allow the client to physically specify how the computing services are provided so substantial control rests with the third-party provider. It is assumed that shared resources will be employed and that the buyer will not have control over the physical environment.

This perceived lack of control over the physical network raises the issue that someone working for the shared service provider might be able to access organization data inappropriately. This is a serious security consideration for most organizations and drives a number of potential adopters to private Clouds.

Private Clouds

Private Clouds are provisioned so that only one organization or entity has control over the infrastructure, and shared resources are solely for the benefit of the organization exerting that control. An example of this may be a private wiki site that only allows access to members of the same corporation.

Private Clouds are under the entity who owns the data's use and control. This definition of private Cloud Computing implies that the entity retains substantial control over the data center and thus sidesteps issues of privacy and security that might deter a financial services firm or a government agency from using Cloud Computing.

This does not mean that the private Cloud has been created or managed by the entity, only that it has substantial control via either contract or ownership of the hosting facilities. This extra control may be simulated as is the case with Google™'s government offering where the data is guaranteed to stay within the confines of the United States and the staffs are subject to extra background checks and security screenings.

For another example, suppose an organization has a collaboration site linking their worldwide research and development group. Since the portal contains engineering documents and discussions between staff on upcoming products, the organization is reluctant to use a public Cloud provider. They can still lease a data center and staff it with contractors, control the process and still maintain this as a private Cloud.

If the information being stored is particularly sensitive, additional precautions such as dedicated physical servers and segregated network connections can be provisioned. This is the quasi private model mentioned previously and will increase the costs but may still be cost-effective compared with provisioning in house.

The disadvantage of private Clouds is that they may not be fully utilized, so compared with public Clouds they may not operate as efficiently.

Community Clouds

A community Cloud is a group united by a common cause or purpose. An example could be a public–private partnership site that hosts collaborative efforts to help airlines improve maintenance practices. Membership is limited to industry and government, but the overall portal is hosted by an industry trade group.

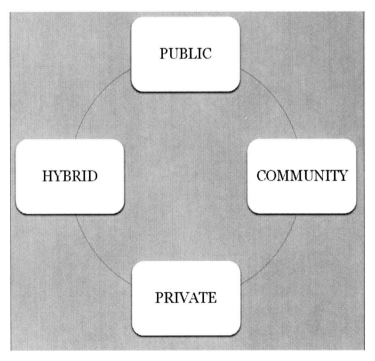

Figure 4: Types of Clouds

Hybrid Clouds share features with the other three models. An example is transportation clearing houses where some information is public, some is private and some may be shared with allied members such as travel booking sites, but not with individual consumers.

SaaS, IaaS and PaaS

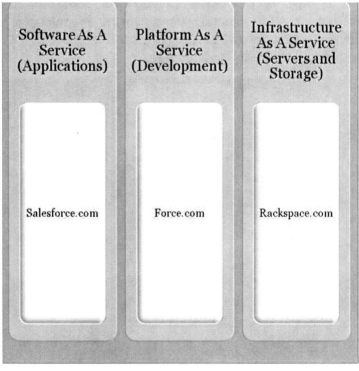

Figure 5: Cloud services

The three generally accepted modes of types of service offered are as follows.

Introduction

Software as a service

Software as a service, or SaaS, provides software applications over the Internet. SaaS provides Cloud-based software services such as customer resources management or enterprise resources management. Another example is office suites in the Clouds, such as Microsoft® Live that duplicates the Microsoft® Office suite for a fee on the Internet.

One early success story of SaaS providers is Salesforce.com, which went online with their flagship customer relationships management suite in 1999. This site keeps track of customer potential sales value (also known as the pipeline), that management can use to manage the sales process, identify profitable sales efforts faster and put more resources into profitable sales contacts. The application suite is growing increasingly sophisticated. Newly arrived is force.com that gives organizations the tools to integrate enterprise systems with Salesforce.com, and produce user-friendly custom dashboards and reports to produce seamless interaction and enhance productivity.

Platform as a service

Platform as a service, or PaaS, provides a development environment. This may seem a bit like SaaS. Technically, I suppose it is, but industry has agreed generally that developers use PaaS and consumers use SaaS.

One example would be a web-hosting platform. Another might be a collaboration platform that provides access to document sharing or video archival and retrieval. Microsoft® Exchange and SharePoint® hosts fall into this category.

Infrastructure as a service

Infrastructure as a service, or IaaS, provides the physical hardware and software required by companies on the Internet. The basic requirement for the consumer is to send a provisioning request for the number of servers with data storage requirements. The servers are provisioned and the access to the servers is granted by the service provider.

IaaS provides a Cloud-based platform for servers, storage, memory, bandwidth and computing power on demand. Typically, the user will need to perform substantial customization of IaaS services. Vendors such as Rackspace and Amazon's EC2 provide servers and storage on demand. The nuances of what applications to use and how to configure the data storage are left to the client.

A sub-class of IaaS is "communications as a service". Vendors such as Vonage and Skype now provide Cloud-based communications using a public Cloud model to provision services. Skype is now offering additional web widgets to provide Skype links on customer service sites.

An additional hurdle for IaaS is the element of applications to configure and manage the service. Google™ Apps and Force.com are examples that provide the ability to customize an existing application and brand it and make it your own. This starts to blur the edges of the "as a service" factor since industry consolidation and the effort to solve more customer problems drives innovation at the edges.

Everything as a service (EaaS) sums up the entire discussion nicely. The main thing to remember is that the Cloud provides services on demand via the network and/or the Internet. What the services are may determine who is using the services, as well as what steps must be taken to reduce risk. The actual labels will become less important over time as the offerings continue to mature.

Disruptive technology

Moving services to the Cloud is disruptive in that the same sorts of service are probably being provided by someone other than the Cloud service provider today. The uncertainty of whether the Cloud represents something new, something old that is being repackaged or something halfway between drives a lot of the angst surrounding the Cloud.

Change usually involves some degree of risk. If we listen to the siren calls of the Cloud service providers, the Cloud is better, faster and cheaper. In much the same way that if you are a hammer, then every problem looks like a nail, the Cloud service providers will provide a Cloud solution to every IT problem.

They are not unified in their approach, their methods or their technology, however. There are as many ways to implement virtualization as there are hardware and software manufacturers. The Cloud may in the long run be the best solution. In the short term, it is much more beneficial to ask what do we want to do before we ask how are we going to do it.

Trusting the Cloud: stop, go or caution

A lot of discussion focuses on securing the Cloud or determining if the Cloud is secure. At a granular level, the Cloud is a compendium of people, processes and technology. The challenge for procurement professionals is determining what questions to ask, what assurances should be in the contracts and how much risk is being assumed when a service is moved to the Cloud.

Cloud services or not, there are definite opportunities opening up. The key is to know which paths are good today for your organization today and which ones are going to be better tomorrow.

Threaded throughout these offerings are IT governance structures to determine how users, applications, hardware and data storage and backup are handled. Because IT is much more complex than other utility offerings like electricity and gas, the details surrounding these offerings are complex as well.

The lines and boundaries dividing the above applications, software, services and infrastructure are constantly shifting, blurring and becoming less distinct. The concept of a Cloud fits this very nicely. Arguing about whether something is PaaS or SaaS seems less important if one can get both from a single provider.

Everything as a service is a model that tries to bridge the remaining gaps between these offerings. By using EaaS as a model, we can evaluate internal *versus* external hosted services for just about everything. If is it better, faster and cheaper, it may be worth a look.

CHAPTER 1: SETTING COURSE TO THE CLOUDS

If you have tried to hire any IT folks lately, you may notice that a) it is difficult to find and keep staff, and b) once you are staffed, they may not always be all that productive. Part of the reason is that the skill set required to put the average organization's IT on the burner is so massive and complex, that the staff may only perform one or two of the critical functions on a monthly basis, not on a weekly basis, much less a daily basis. As a result, when you hear of a computer installation gone wrong or having to scratch something and start over "now that we have it right," there is a common theme: core competencies.

You don't develop competence by performing something every week or so. You have to live, sleep, eat and drink in a functional area before you can really take on the mantle of guru. So for the less frequently performed tasks, there is an assumption that the low-volume player will be outshone by the high-volume player, given the same game. Gurus get to be gurus by talent and training, not talent alone.

If you think of managing an IT system, the core issues are the same for every organization. If you have to upgrade a system from one version to another frequently, the next one starts to get a bit easier. If you are running the same application for multiple organizations, then you are likely to discover ways to run that application better. That leads to repeatability and, from the standpoint of Capability

Maturity Model (CMM)® Integration, repeatability takes you up the scale of quality and reduces the risk of mistakes.

In the transportation business, a lorry driver who runs a dedicated route is less likely to have an accident. The reason is that by running the same route every day, the driver becomes familiar with the terrain.

The same principle applies to systems. The installation gets easier the second time through. If you have to install the same kind of system hundreds of times, the route is familiar and there are fewer reasons for errors.

There are equivalent dedicated runs in IT today. Each organization has things that they are great at and that they do all the time. There are other jobs they do less frequently. If we can focus on the functions they don't have to be great at and that they perform less frequently, and there is a viable, externally available replacement service, this function may fall into the commodity functional level, ripe for outsourcing and perhaps moving to the Cloud.

Renting *versus* owning infrastructure

How many times have you purchased a PC, a laptop or even a cell phone, only to find something similar with more features, better performance and lower cost within a few months or even weeks of purchase?

Moore's law postulates that computing performance would double processing power every 18 months. Based on this

---

® CMM is registered in the US Patent and Trademark Office by Carnegie Mellon University.

premise, why are we investing in infrastructure on a three-or four-year cycle that will be outdated in 18 months?

This question is complicated by the fact that an IT department doesn't just buy one box; they buy hundreds or thousands at a time, every one exhibiting the same sort of ticking infrastructure countdown.

The staff levels, the support applications and hardware deployed to support equipment and infrastructure are growing right along with the number of boxes an organization supports.

Another issue to consider is depth on the bench. If your organization has one really good server lead person, what happens if that one leaves or gets sick? Maybe you hire a second server person as a backup. But now, with two individuals doing the same function, they may not have the volume to stay busy 100% of the time. So you give one of them 75% servers and 25% help desk support.

Small to medium-sized businesses can't keep up with this model so they frequently augment staff with contractor support. No issue here except you have just backed into a shared service model. The contractor resources are no longer dedicated staff. They can provide surge support but may not be available full time.

Contrasting these challenges with Cloud infrastructure, the boxes are set up in real time. There is no upfront capital expense. If a server fails, the Cloud provider takes care of any hardware issues at their end and will have the capacity to immediately stage replacement equipment without the weeks to months of lead time associated with a capital infrastructure investment.

Scalability

When infrastructure owners need more equipment, they have to make sure they have the people, space and power to support it. Then starting from a plan, they go to budget, purchase authorization, order, track, installation, payment and operations.

In the Cloud realm, you sign up for an account, specify resources needed, order, and within minutes the server is available. The server provisioning creates a rental or chargeback ticket and you're done.

The heaviest part of the physical infrastructure bother – the staff requirements, perhaps a bit of the technological risk, and that the next best thing will be half again as expensive – has been effectively bottled.

From this, I hope it is clear why the Cloud seems to be gaining momentum. As they say, the devil is in the details, so there are some caveats and there are as many alternate paths to this utopian ideal as there are paths to the dystopian depths. So let's see how to find the right path, shall we?

The larger they are, the less likely they are to fall

This may be a bit of a surprise, but the bigger the organization, the less they may benefit from outsourcing their services, since larger organizations have purchasing power and internal production costs that approach or even surpass all but the largest Cloud service providers.

Smaller organizations may not have the inherent staff and controls to duplicate a Cloud environment in-house cost-effectively. There is also a risk that the internal staff may not be able to master the Cloud technology without some training and outside assistance.

In a larger organization, there are still benefits from adopting Cloud architecture, also referred to as a private Cloud. There are still economies and efficiencies to be gained from consolidating workload and reducing the time from initiation to deployment. In some cases, by using Cloud provisioning techniques, organizations are reporting a four-month gain in productivity over previous methods.

The majority of these gains are likely to be from two sources, one being the use of virtualization to create virtual copies of physical servers. The virtual copy works the same as a physical server; it has the same interfaces and capabilities. The difference is that the virtual server is one of dozens of similar servers running on a single physical device.

The other is the elimination of procurement for a single device. Since centralized procurement of the hosting physical server is already complete, a request for a virtual server can be handled similarly to a request for a new user id or an e-mail account; no funds have to change hands, everything happens in cyberspace and it is only the delay from a provisioning standpoint that has any effect on the process.

Going virtual

Virtualization technology is still relatively new as commercial off-the-shelf software. It is getting easier to deploy, but professional services companies exist for a reason. If your organization does not have the staff training and skill set, it might be better to bring in some experienced consulting staff to oversee installation of a private Cloud environment or help configure and integrate a public Cloud environment.

Cloud platforms and rapid system prototyping

The benefit of this rapid provisioning in Cloud environments can be seen very clearly in the ability to set up a test system rapidly and in isolation from the corporate network. Testing is seen as onerous by some programmers, so the easier you make it for them to start and document their testing, the easier it is for the organization to mandate compliance.

The cost of providing hardware for the developers can be much less expensive in a Cloud environment. Systems can be configured, used for a time and then the resources dissolved back into the Cloud once the project is completed. There is no capital expense, and rapid configuration can shave weeks or months off costs by eliminating hardware procurement and replacing it with a metered utility Cloud platform rental model that may be pre-approved for an operational surge in capacity requirements.

Partially configured test systems have been used to attack corporate networks. Since they may be connected prior to being completely configured, they may be vulnerable to attack and can get infected by malware. If the infection is undetected, the system can be used as a launching pad for other attacks on the network. By loading test systems off "gold" copy images of the corporate operating system, the servers already have the required patches installed and are less vulnerable to attack.

Consolidating low-use applications

If there are low-use applications that require a server, but may not require all of the resources, they can now be consolidated onto one system that is divided into sections called virtual machines.

Each virtual machine will perform and appear in the system environment to be the same as a unique physical server. The difference is that the virtual machine can be started up and taken down without affecting the operation of the physical machine.

Instead of a dedicated server running all the time in a wiring closet, the application can sleep away waiting for the uptick in demand to awaken a call for more resources. In the meantime, other servers with more pressing demands can use the full power of the machine until it is again time to share with their less demanding brethren.

Patch management services

Another benefit of shared service models and virtualization is enhanced patch management. Patches are updates to system software that correct programming mistakes and enhance security.

By patching the "golden" copies of the server, all of the new virtual devices that boot up based on the newly patched system are also patched.

Security does not accrue from doing nothing; it erodes. The number of exploits generally goes up for a particular version of the software. If the organization does not maintain an active and vigilant patching and software maintenance campaign, it is only a matter of time before these vulnerabilities come home to roost.

In the fall of 2008 and early spring of 2009, a software worm called Conficker spread rapidly around the world. The irony is that the original vulnerability the system used to spread was patched by Microsoft$^®$ in November 2008.

Theoretically, any system patched after this date would not catch or attempt to spread the Conficker malware. The reported number of systems infected worldwide was 5 to 10 million at its peak. This represents not the total number of unpatched systems, but the total number of unpatched or otherwise vulnerable machines that were infected.

The number of unpatched vulnerable machines is likely to be quite higher. The point of the five million number is that a significant portion of these computers were not patched.

QualSys calls this the vulnerability half life.

("Qualsys reveals Laws of Vulnerabilities 2.0 declarations", InfoSecurity Europe.
www.qualys.com/company/newsroom/newsreleases/uk/vie w/2009•04•28/.)

In 2003, when they first started gathering statistics, they found it took an average of 30 days to patch half of the vulnerable systems. In 2008, they found industry had only reduced this figure to 29.5 days! This gives the advantage to computer hackers, who have an open season of at least 29.5 days to attack and try to take advantage of the unpatched machines.

By changing the technology over to virtual, the process of patching becomes a bit easier and faster. Patch once, reload the servers and all are now patched. It is also easier to test patches.

Cloud backup

Even if you are not ready to take the plunge for moving applications, there are so many services running in the Cloud that something will likely be useful. Disaster recovery/data storage in the Cloud will allow databases to be backed up to lower-cost Cloud storage vendors.

Consumer services such as Mozy and Seagate's Internet drive are already in this space for consumers. Mozy is now offering a 2 GB free consumer account and larger data storage is available for a few dollars a month. The same features and more are available for enterprise users. These can take the form of simply configuring disks to store backups, all the way up to full-blown replication environments that can be switched on as production environments in the event of a problem.

This is one stop short of fully converting to the Cloud environment for processing. It may serve as a useful waypoint towards fully embracing Cloud Computing.

Cloud bursting: surge capacity

If the organization needs seasonal surges in storage or processing capacity, using the Cloud as the peak capacity source can lower the high-water mark of processing capacity required by the organization. This is called Cloud bursting. The surge capacity is rented while you use it at quite reasonable rates, and it does not require a great deal of time or skill to set up.

Amazon is in this space with their Simple Storage Solution (S3), and their recent announcement of the Amazon virtual private Cloud, which allows a secure encrypted tunnel between the enterprise and the Amazon Cloud, may increase enterprise adoption of their service.

Desktop office suites

Desktop apps such as Microsoft® SharePoint®, Exchange and Live Meeting can be rented off the Cloud. This may reduce the overall cost of implementation. Microsoft® also has similar offerings with Windows® Live.

The Microsoft® Office suite Cloud offering is launching as a commercial product. By moving to a desktop software rental, gone are the days of one box running 2003 while another gets 2007. When the Cloud upgrades, all of the clients instantly upgrade as well.

The amount of internal angst and processing cycles required to manage this in an organization of 10,000 desktops makes such apps worth serious consideration.

Symphony

IBM has rebranded OpenOffice under the Symphony trademark. Their most recent update includes extensions to integrate with SharePoint® 2007. Previously, you had to run Microsoft® Office 2007 to gain full document control and check out capability.

Zoho Office for SharePoint®

Zoho offers a Cloud-based office suite with the desktop apps to edit and collaborate hosted on Zoho's servers. The documents can sit behind the organization's firewall hosted on SharePoint® to retain control over the information.

Google™ Docs

Google™ Docs also provide online documents presence. For US$50 per person per year, the organization gains access to a host of user productivity applications. The data and the application reside in the Cloud, are backed up, and provide some nifty collaboration features. Another upside is little or no maintenance.

You might even provision open source Linux® on your desktops to access these via Mozilla®/Firefox® browsers. This may reduce the overall cost of desktops by exchanging a capital expense model for desktop apps with the groovy Cloud-based rental model.

An additional benefit for all of the above is portability. If you access your documents at work and now must travel, you still have the same access at home or at an Internet café as you have in the office. The only requirement is the availability of Internet access.

Crowdsourcing and social networking

Services such as blogs, wikis and news feeds can be consolidated into one site to link together a community with a shared purpose to collaborate on solutions or simply offer ideas and suggestions for mutual interest.

Options for hosting collaboration portals range from SharePoint® and Adobe® Connect™ on the enterprise software side, to Google™ Wave and Wikipedia® on the "everything is on the network anyway" Cloud approach.

The benefits of moving from a single subject-matter expert to a crowd of subject-matter experts has to be balanced against the sensitivity of the question being asked and the willingness of the crowd to answer. In the case of Apps for Democracy (see below), the combination of prizes and social activism seemed to deliver a wealth of worthy suggestions.

The key here is that the incentives for responding may need to be carefully considered along with a safe harbor for participants should the solutions run counter to the current party line. Once you start promoting openness in an organization, be careful that the openness doesn't have to be restrained.

A case in point is one organization which opened up a blog for customers. Shortly thereafter, social activists started posting to the site. Since the posts were not moderated, i.e. reviewed by an administrator before they appeared in public, the site had to be taken down because of the negative publicity generated.

Rules of engagement should be decided before launching the site, enough resources need to be available to support it, and consideration of the consequences if too much sharing takes place should be clearly understood and communicated to participants beforehand.

Used in a corporate environment, this can be a powerful tool to link experts, create repositories of institutional knowledge and provide critical mass to solve problems.

The city of DC under the guidance of Vivek Kundra created a site called Apps for Democracy. The proposal was simple: 30 days, US$50,000 in prize money. The request: suggestions and applications to help the city provide web services.

The result: 47 applications, US$2,300,000 in value and only US$50,000 disbursed. A second run of the same competition requesting applications in 2009 yielded 230 insights or suggestions, a similar number of applications and only US$30,000 disbursed.

The winning application allowed the user to report problems such as broken street lamps or potholes on an iPhone™ app or Facebook®, track the problem resolution and see where the reporter ranked with all reporters in the hall of fame. The prize money awarded to the winner was US$12,000. Not a bad return on investment.

Similar services for reverse auction sites post contractor assignments online. Service providers bid on the contracts and the best proposal wins.

The operating system

Virtual desktops have the advantage of allowing the user to boot up from a golden image of the operating system (OS). No virus can penetrate the golden image so each virtual session will erase any viruses or malware that manages to infect any previous sessions. Normally, once a computer has been infected, it will stay infected until the system is manually purged of the virus or malware or the system is rebuilt from scratch. In the case of using a virtual desktop, the system starts from scratch every day from this golden image, so the viruses and malware that used to lurk undetected for weeks or months will only persist for the current session. This reduces the effectiveness of the attack because the infection does not last as long in a virtual desktop environment.

One such virtual desktop vendor is Citrix®. Citrix® is designed to host a Windows® or Linux® desktop accessible via a web browser. The desktop work is performed in the Cloud data center; the web client communicates screen updates from the remote machine back to the browser, and remote keystrokes and mouse clicks back to the host system. The advantage is total control over the hosted desktop; a follow-me desktop that doesn't change even if the user logs in from home, the office or the road.

Because IT staff have physical control of the desktop, they can patch to their heart's content and lock down the settings on the desktop to harden it against attacks and if there is a problem with the user, it usually stops at the desktop browser in terms of support. This may reduce support costs. The downside is the increase in license costs associated with the Citrix® software.

Green computing: power and the grid

Running a data center requires huge capital investments, not only in computing power, but also gensets, uninterruptible power supplies (UPSs) and engineering support. By moving to a shared or managed service environment, the data center does not have to be located on site, the gensets and UPS can be repurposed and the cost per transaction is driven down.

In practice, setting up virtual servers and expecting instant surge capacity is a bit unrealistic. The actual servers have to be created, booted and ready to process transactions. This means that idle capacity is idle capacity, Cloudy or not. Cloud Computing consolidates workloads on high-performance multicore processors running virtualization software.

Virtualization software allows for a single application server to be broken into fractional replicas called virtual machines. The software allows for granular control of processing resources and can reallocate processing power between virtual machines based on demand. This feature also allows each virtual machine to appear to have a unique configuration, list of authorized users, and identity.

This configuration runs more efficiently than a single stand-alone server that might be limited to a single set of users and one configuration.

Based on this technology, as the utilization of each physical server goes up, the cost of processing each user session goes down. This consolidation reduces the server footprint; it may increase cooling needs but overall power consumption drops. Automation of server creation and provisioning reduces the amount of staff time required for support, since one physical server now can take on the workload of 30 to 40 physical servers.

Consolidation of low-use applications, with easier cloning of test environments, reduces power consumption. With the continued drive to increase processor power, Moore's law said that on average every 18 months, the power and capacity would double. Sure enough, he has been right all along. With this power, and the power of virtualization, the Cloud will come to us.

Additional macro forces are starting to take hold and gain traction for the green data-center movement. One is to locate data centers on top of the least expensive abundant power sources such as hydro. Another is to locate them in cooler climes such as Minnesota and Canada. Each has its proponents, but this trend will surely continue to fuel consolidation and the shared service model.

Major benefits of Cloud Computing

To summarize, there are many benefits to embracing Cloud Computing and the managed shared service model. For every benefit, there are also likely to be caveats. No one-size-fits-all solution exists today (vendor hype excepted), just as no two organizations are alike. In the following chapters, we will start to address some of these caveats as well.

Core competencies of the data center staff

As we stated previously, when a task is repeated daily, the skill levels increase at a rapid rate. Generational best practices can be discovered and innovation peaks. By contrast, if the data center staff have to perform similar tasks once per quarter, there is lower incentive to innovate.

By concentrating infrastructure, the Cloud service provider can also afford more esoteric specialists to support the sales and engineering effort. This can translate into on-demand support models, automation of tools and processes, or consultative relationships in order to move legacy applications to the Cloud.

This may be most beneficial in an environment with a shrinking market share, such as mainframe or mini-computer support. Accessing contracted help online may provide staff surges in critical areas without having to bring in staff on a permanent basis to support system conversions. Once done, the consultant goes away. Once hired, the same may not be true for IT specialists ...

Increased utilization

In spite of the huge cost, the average server is only in use for 10 to 20% of the time, then waiting for something to do. When you share systems among more users, the utilization can increase dramatically. According to Intel®, the performance gain from a server refresh that consolidates workload *versus* systems that were in place four years ago is 10:1.

By using a shared service model, more users can access the same system and the idle capacity is reduced.

This means that:

- You won't have to grow the data center at the same pace.
- Less power will be consumed.
- There will be less of an impact on the environment.
- Surge capacity will be available as needed.

Because the Cloud provider has excess capacity, when a spike in processing requires more resources, the consumer can simply draw more computing power. In a private computing center, this excess capacity may also exist but must be planned for. Cloud environments are built on a much larger scale and again, as a core competency, will also stay ahead of the capacity curve so that the average company could look at the capacity as nearly limitless.

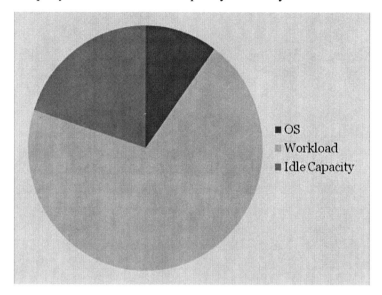

Figure 6: Average server utilization with virtualization

24/7 watch centers

Staffing is expensive. With shared services, staffing is spread among wider populations. Smaller businesses have to rely on remote sensing and automated monitors to watch data centers. Some thresholds may be too low to be noticed by these automated systems until it is too late. By maintaining a mixture of automated and human controls, larger entities can react quickly to emerging events, even when the manager is just getting paged out of bed.

Enhanced recovery through server and data replication

Server and data replication uses hardware to create backup images of servers and data to a remote site. This is not an advantage restricted only to the Cloud, but it is an increasingly popular option now that many data storage vendors build support for this function into their management software. If the hosted service provider uses similar hardware, they can easily host your remote data in their Cloud data center. This certainly can reduce the amount of data lost between backups if there is a catastrophic failure.

Free staff time

By using a shared service model, the current IT staff can be repurposed. All of the staffing required to support infrastructure can be moved to more customer-focused, rather than technology-focused, tasks.

Capital expenses replaced with operational expenses

The cost per transaction will be reduced by outsourcing. Growth of IT infrastructure and the resulting headaches can be slowed and then reversed. Significant amounts of the infrastructure in place will go away, but there are learning curves in transitioning to new technology. The remaining infrastructure will likely go to end of life at the same pace as before. The difference will show up in the equipment refresh, when less new equipment will need to be purchased to replace retiring equipment. The benefit is still there. In traditional outsourcing agreements and private Cloud models, there may be options to do a purchase/leaseback to get the equipment off the books faster by transferring ownership to the service provider.

External certification and quality of service

External organizations may hold themselves to a higher standard in order to meet certification requirements. The incentive for a company performing a service for hire *versus* performing in-house as a captive department is striking. Service providers build service-oriented models in order to comply with contractual service level agreements. Internal providers may not have the same incentive.

There is momentum building for internal adoption of such certifications as well because of the impact of privacy laws and compliance with regulatory requirements such as Sarbanes-Oxley. This focus on customer service should accelerate as more of the infrastructure transitions to a Cloud model.

The cost of certification would be borne by the provider's customer base, not necessarily the organization. By certifying a data center process for hire, the cost is shared among all of the tenants of the data center. Thus the acquisition of an ISO27001 certified service may be much less expensive outside the corporate confines than if purchased in house.

CHAPTER 2: PREFLIGHT CHECK

A US government CIO when asked, "Assuming that the Cloud is the future for a lot of current computing functions, what can an organization do now to prepare and future-proof their organization?" replied, "Find out what you have. That is the best place to start".

So, from that, we begin a discussion of your computing architecture. Architecture may seem a bit boring. Enterprise architects analyze and document the current system design, starting with a high level of how systems are connected, burrowing down into the application connections and sometimes even the connections within an application. Understanding the current environment is an important first step to changing it for the better. Once finished, as with painting the Golden Gate Bridge, it is time to start over.

In other words, identifying what legacy applications you have is the first step to identifying how, and if, they will run in the Cloud. Some may take years of reengineering before conversion; others may be retired as new processes take their place in the Cloud.

The main point is that this is how your organization can begin to think strategically about what the Cloud is, what benefits it offers and from there, what would be a good, relatively painless way to start migrating some functions to the Cloud and once done, document that it has some benefit.

Starting with an enterprise applications overview and inventory generates multiple dividends:

- Applications can be identified that might be otherwise overlooked.
- The global enterprise inventory may shed light on areas ripe for consolidation.
- Connections and interdependencies that may affect implementation can be identified so the project manager can develop the project timeline.

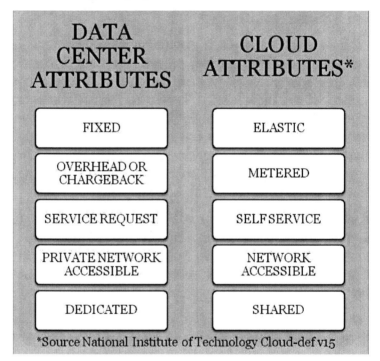

Figure 7: Cloud attributes

Computing as a utility

Capacity planning is one of the most grueling exercises for data center managers. Get it wrong and either it is too slow or underutilized. Seldom will it be just right. Even if it is just right, that may mean that it is only just right until the organization surges again and you drop back to too slow.

Elasticity

The beauty of the Cloud model is that all resources are consolidated. It is likely that some of the users will be idle and there will be very few instances where everyone is at peak usage at the same time. This is very much like the telecom utilities. There were seldom enough lines for everyone to talk at the same time, but simply enough to cover the highest average number of conversations during the month.

This ability to provide on-demand bandwidth and computing power is driven by the excess capacity built into the Cloud. As long as the Cloud provider engineers for the rapid expansion and anticipates growth, the Cloud users will have the illusion of unlimited capacity.

In a public Cloud, this pushes more of the risk onto the Cloud provider who has to make the hardware investments. The Cloud users can surge-process month-end or quarter-end reports, then return to a lower baseline usage throughout the month.

In a private Cloud, this consolidates all of the hardware into a resource pool for the organization. This consolidation may reduce the risk because a larger resource pool will proportionately be able to handle more transactions than the same amount of hardware in separate resource pools. The reason is that some resources will be idle in individual pools, yet be unable to share these spare cycles with the aggregate demand.

Capacity requirements

Previously, a captive data center would have to invest in enough hardware to cover the high-water mark of processing. This would have to be done far in advance of when it might be needed. This adds to the uncertainty and may contribute to over-purchasing of hardware to avoid capacity constraints.

Now this is covered by a service agreement with the Cloud provider, and the organization will only have to pay for what it uses. Once the usage drops, so does the meter.

Baseline service levels

Measure the current state or baseline quality and service levels the organization is experiencing before you convert to the service provider. Understanding where you are when starting out will be important for measuring the value of the end product.

This is also a good issue to start talking about with the potential service providers. If they understand your current process has a sub-second response time, they will either need to adjust accordingly or communicate why they may not be able to meet the same benchmark.

The better you can articulate your expectations beforehand, the more likely the overall end product will match your expectations. If the vendor cannot meet your expectations, hopefully they will be able to tell you in advance before you commit to using them.

In-sourcing

The definition of in-sourcing is to use an internal resource to provide a service. A sister organization may be quite competent at e-mail and web hosting, while another may do payroll. A third may have access to the full financial suite of a major enterprise resource planning (ERP) vendor. The workload is passed to the area of the global organization that has demonstrated the best core competency. In the US government space, this is normally referred to as line of business services or LOB.

The opportunities for your organization to use the Cloud environment to link the global organization efficiently to the best of services will be unique to your organization. Benefits may accrue from consolidation and centralization of procurement. Retiring legacy systems to concentrate on a single replacement system or simply moving all of the payroll functions to one business unit may suffice. The main point is that recognizing who has the best software and platform for particular procedures can break down some of the corporate barriers, free resources and reduce future expenditures.

Targeting legacy systems

If the vendor no longer supports particular software, continuing to hang on to an older version can open up rifts of vulnerabilities. This may be the case where the application was written for one version of a database provider such as Oracle®. If the database application is not updated and patched, your application may be at risk if vulnerabilities are discovered and publicized.

Some may make the argument that security via obscurity will keep data safe. I disagree. There are too many bad actors out there to assume they will not find your vulnerability; it only a question of when they will find it.

While synchronizing the retirement of systems with replacement by Cloud systems may be a worthy goal, the main issue at hand is not the technology; it is the process by which you evaluate the technology and the people you have at your disposal. There may be some hidden barriers to conversion and subtle or not-so-subtle resistance to change.

Planning for staff transition

Another issue that is buried in the human resources (HR) function of many organizations is that the training and upkeep of IT staff require that they spend considerable time and expense in lifelong learning and pursuit of the latest techniques to support enterprise systems.

In small to medium-sized organizations, training may be relegated to the back burner while the latest fire is put out. Over time, the core competencies will coalesce around the putting out of fires and not necessarily around the latest and greatest techniques for server deployment.

This may reduce the role that the legacy staff can play in converting to the new platform. However, there is a genuine risk that the staff may leave prior to the conversion being completed if the organization fails to clearly define a new role for them post conversion. This can not only complicate the conversion, it can also sink it if there is no one available who can understand the functionality of the legacy system.

Avoiding self-inflicted wounds

More than one organization has completely shut down their e-mail due to configuration or backup problems. Most of these failures track back to lack of staff training or test resources. If you accept that the nature of e-mail and web hosting is a commodity business, it may make more sense to outsource this sort of application in order to concentrate on issues that really differentiate the organization, such as applications development and business process engineering.

In larger organizations, some measure of training is usually formally mandated. Job descriptions may require third-party certifications and mandatory continuing education. Research and development groups and internal labs are set up to test hardware and software improvements. The degree of separation from these internal groups in larger organizations and those providing external hosting may be negligible. This means the staff will likely understand the new technology and can take a more active role in the conversion.

The point is, it is important to consider the human element in these conversions. Maintaining an adequate forward-leaning HR plan to redeploy staff post conversion is key to their retention and may reduce the risk that key staff will leave before the job is completed.

Economies of scale

The purchasing power of larger organizations may meet or surpass that of third-party hosts. Smaller or medium-sized organizations without the maturity level of their larger brethren may find it beneficial to explore public Cloud

Computing in order to reduce the dependency on privately hosted services.

As the saying goes, one-offs always cost more, so if the deployment of an Microsoft® Exchange or WebMail server is not done every day, consider pushing some of this outside the organization. If there are pressing security concerns such as "then they would have access to our e-mail," it may be prudent to consider that by default so do most of the Internet service providers. There are options to encrypt e-mail at the client level to reduce this risk across the board for the more sensitive employees.

Bigger pipes are better

An additional wrinkle in today's more aggressive security operating environment is that by positioning your e-mail and web hosting in the Cloud, it may be more secure due to the larger bandwidths available by sitting directly on top of a fiber connection to the Internet.

Distributed denial-of-service (DDoS) attacks use corrupted machines called zombies or bots to attack other machines. The zombies generally are programmed to work together in what is called a botnet. When zombies in a botnet are ordered to attack one server or network, they can have the devastating effect of flooding that network with so much false traffic that the system stops performing and legitimate users are prevented or denied service.

These types of denial-of-service (DoS) attacks are simple to launch and difficult to defend against. Some botnets like Conficker have infected over five million machines simultaneously.

One security provider has said that one of the most effective defenses is to have a multi-gigabit Internet pipe to simply ride out the attacks. Not many organizations can afford a 10GB pipe just sitting idle waiting for a DDoS attack. However, if this pipe is a shared commodity, such as is the case in the Cloud, the cost to the organization can be shared among so many users that the cost becomes negligible.

Moving big iron (mainframes) to the Clouds

Of course, the options are endless and the selection quite probably is unique to your group. One area that is seldom explored, since it doesn't seem at first be a Cloud technology, is pure mainframe and mini outsourcing. Virtualization cut its teeth on mainframe time shares. In the interim, the mainframe has gotten even more powerful and concentrating mini-computers and mainframes in the Cloud and sharing them among many organizations may be a cost-effective alternative to maintaining your own data center.

Virtualization is supported on nearly every platform, not just the small server environment. Consider the possibility that the organization could benefit from a shared service model.

Using the iSeries® or Zseries® mainframes as examples, the older versions of these systems supported a couple of thousand simultaneous users. Now the top-end boxes support not only thousands of users but also can run multiple virtual environments with users and transactional capacity for many thousands more.

If your organization is supporting an iSeries® or Zseries® mainframe, it may have a dedicated staff simply to keep up with patching and hand-holding. By looking at a remotely hosted version, you may be able to put these staff on more critical work. At the same time, you may be able to take advantage of advanced replication techniques available to the largest shops. This could reduce or flatten your overall expenditure while at the same time improving performance and overall availability.

Storage in the Cloud

Storage in the Cloud is now becoming a ubiquitous commodity. Previously, a connection between a server and the data storage required a physical connection. The evolution of protocols such as iSCSI and iSATA are allowing data storage to reside across the network in another state, province or even country.

Using a process called replication, as soon as the data is written, it can also be copied to a remote device. This provides a high level of fault tolerance and can reduce the amount of data lost if a system is disrupted to only seconds worth. The remote system is often fitted with a tape backup device in order to provide yet another level of redundancy. Too many tales of "I didn't think it was necessary" have been told for the redundancy issue to be ignored.

By replicating the data and the processing capacity in the Cloud, if one system goes dark, the redundant system can pick up in rotation. The complexity of such real-time replication used to be quite daunting to the average small or medium-sized business (SMB), but the benefits often reserved for the largest entities are now within reach through these mechanisms, and SMBs should consider taking advantage of these now.

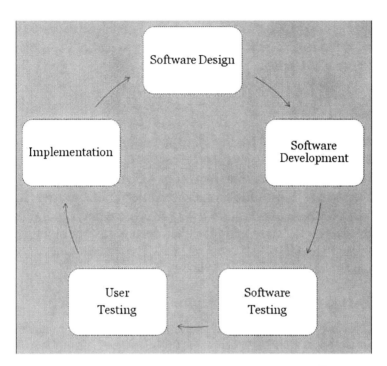

Figure 8: Software development life cycle

Bandwidth and try it before you buy it

When moving applications to the Cloud, the end-users will need enough bandwidth to access not only their legacy applications but also the Cloud-based applications. Without proper planning, this may result in lower service levels and lead to an early demise of the system. To avoid this, consider including testing as a requirement in your service level agreement.

Testing can simulate a normal production environment by creating transactions automatically that duplicate the data entry for hundreds of thousands of users. The results can be used to adjust the project, reduce the number of users while infrastructure catches up, or simply to cancel a project before it is too late.

Instant test beds

Another feature of having all of the computing resources at the developer's disposal is the ability to rapidly provision and create test environments. The value of this cannot be overstated. More than one implementation project has failed because of a lack of testing and some portion of these go back to the inability to secure a suitable test environment.

Reduce the scope of the implementation

This last may not be used enough, considering the number of projects that fail to meet initial expectations, but by adjusting the initial number of users and providing both a Cloud and a legacy method to achieve the same results, the project manager can lower the risk of the implementation.

Testing can identify areas of concern that an organization may not readily identify until there is the duress and chaos caused by a full premature implementation. It is much better to discover these issues under limited engagements than to blaze ahead and find out with the entire enterprise at risk.

Pod computing reduces configuration time

One trend that may reduce some of the angst is pod computing. Pods are preconfigured clustered racks of servers; all are configured the same way by the manufacturer or an integrator.

When a new server is ordered, it is in the form of a fully configured rack including power distribution, disk and network switches. It is rolled in as a unit and will only need to have the operating image applied to move into production. Although this does not absolve the organization from capacity planning, it does reduce the time needed to install hardware once it arrives at the data center.

The average data center is too complicated. If your data center manager knows where all of the cables go, everything is labeled, and they can pull up a raised floor tile anywhere in the center and it all looks basically the same, you are in the minority.

If all the servers are the same, if all the apps are on the same platform, if all of the techs are trained to about the same level of expertise – but life is just not that orderly. But if you can move these apps and ops to the Cloud, it may start to look more orderly.

Since the Cloud provider is basically selling the one size fits all, by default they are most likely going to buy a lot of the same sorts of equipment, run it all the same way, and follow the same paths to set up boxes and containers.

In a way, the economies of scale guarantee a certain amount of stability in the Cloud. So if your applications fit this environment, it may be worth investigating. Consider adopting a framework for development, such as a service-oriented architecture model that specifies that application developers must follow common guidelines. This makes it easier to share code and to leverage each developer's efforts.

Project management *versus ad hoc*

Project management is repeatable; it has stakeholder buy in, good communications, a firm set of agreed upon objectives, and a formal method to adjust those objectives and to communicate expectations and estimates of time and level of effort back to stakeholders, so that they have enough facts to make decisions and support the various outcomes of the project.

Getting better at execution is one of the promised outcomes of Cloud Computing. Let us home in on the approach path to make sure everyone arrives in time and in one piece!

Elasticity reduces need for capacity planning

For capacity planning, a public Cloud inherently has excess capacity. A private Cloud may still need to look carefully at capacity planning in order to anticipate the needs and requirements of the private Cloud infrastructure. It is also important to look at the options and fallback scenarios in case the launch produces some unintended consequences.

Calculating cost benefit

Cloud services fall into many categories. From consolidating applications, consolidating hardware, and consolidating services to consolidating platforms, the key to understanding the Cloud is understanding your own requirements.

If service is paramount, imagine what would happen in its absence. If transactions must be consummated on time, imagine what would happen in a delay. One of the first issues with outsourcing anything is that the only leverage you will have with your Cloud service provider starts with legal leverage. This may not be a consolation if the partner selected cannot perform for some reason.

Justification for taking any risk has to be balanced with the reward.

Before any real decision is required:

- Determine whether you really do have the requisite understanding of your organization.
- Look at each system within the portfolio of all systems to determine if any of them meet the criteria for a Cloud environment.
- If so, take the next steps to determine what a successful conversion would look like.

Can the conversion be made while keeping the legacy system intact?

Are there candidates for Cloud backup and recovery?

Backup and recovery could meet some financial goals by providing lower-cost alternatives to traditional hot-site recovery vendors and establishing benchmarks and metrics for future Cloud projects. Since this is a secondary site, the performance issues are secondary in a recovery scenario, where great performance is measured in minutes and good performance in hours.

In truth, there will be no one answer that will fit all situations. The main concerns are moving forward towards what may be the best way to reduce operational costs in the next decade.

At the same time, if neither your external provider nor internal staff can provide the requisite performance, there are genuine risks to an enterprise if a mission-critical application is selected and the transit, security, capacity and performance are not all in synch.

For this reason, many organizations select applications development and testing as the first Cloud project. The developers are technically competent, a bit more forgiving on hiccups, and will likely provide better, faster feedback if it is not working.

Two other suitable applications are e-mail and web hosting. These are selected primarily because they are generally commodity applications and it is not difficult to communicate the *status quo* operating parameters to an external entity for duplication.

There have been some documented cases where the external providers have had problems. Consider adopting disaster recovery language and specific methods of testing in the service level agreement before committing to outsourcing these functions.

CHAPTER 3: TAXI RUNWAY

Start-up risks

The data centers of today have some great capabilities. It is nearly free to connect one, it is much easier to start one up and it may not take all that much care and feeding once it is established.

That can translate into lots of folks offering you a bit of their Cloud, like Amazon's EC2 service. And if some of the more dodgy start-ups (Amazon excepted, of course) haven't done their homework, their Cloud could spring a hole and deflate. That puts you, your organization and maybe everyone else that you do business with at risk.

Choosing a service provider

With all of these standards, competing offerings, and competing Cloud models, what service provider should I choose?

Before we can answer that question, we again need to look towards the architecture of the existing enterprise. What are the typical data center options in use by the organization today?

- E-mail
- Web hosting
- Collaboration
- Blogs and wikis
- Document management
- Data storage
- Online backup.

Types of Cloud services

Software as a service

Software as a service (SaaS) provides Cloud-based software services such as customer resources management or enterprise resources management. Another example is office suites in the Clouds such as Microsoft® Live that duplicates the Microsoft® Office suite for a fee on the Internet.

One early success story of SaaS providers is Salesforce.com. This site keeps track of customer contact management and is growing increasingly sophisticated. Newly arrived is Force.com that gives organizations the tools to integrate enterprise systems with Salesforce.com to produce seamless interaction and enhance productivity.

Platform as a service

Platform as a service (PaaS) provides a Cloud-based platform such as e-mail, web serving, and collaboration. One example would be a web-hosting platform. Another might be a collaboration platform that provides access to developer tools, document sharing, online slide decks or video archival and retrieval. Microsoft® Exchange and SharePoint® hosts fall into this category.

A sub-class of PaaS is "communications as a service". Vendors such as Vonage and Skype now provide Cloud-based communications using a public Cloud model to provision services. Skype is now offering additional web widgets to provide Skype links on customer service sites.

An additional hurdle for PaaS is the element of applications to configure and manage the service. Google™ Apps and Force.com are examples that provide the ability to customize an existing application, brand it and make it your own.

Infrastructure as a service

Infrastructure as a service (IaaS) provides a Cloud-based platform for servers, storage, memory, bandwidth and computing power on demand. Typically, the user will need to perform substantial customization of IaaS services. Vendors such as Rackspace provide servers and storage on demand. The nuances of what applications to use and how to configure the data storage are left to the client.

Threaded throughout these offerings are IT governance structures to determine how users, applications, hardware, data storage and backup are handled. Because IT is much more complex than other utility offerings like electricity and gas, the details surrounding these offerings are complex as well.

Everything as a service

The lines and boundaries dividing the above applications, software, services and infrastructure are constantly shifting, blurring and becoming less distinct. The concept of a Cloud fits this very nicely. Everything as a service (EaaS) is a model that tries to bridge the remaining gaps between these offerings. By using EaaS as a model, we can evaluate internal *versus* external hosted services for just about everything.

Risk assessment and gap analysis

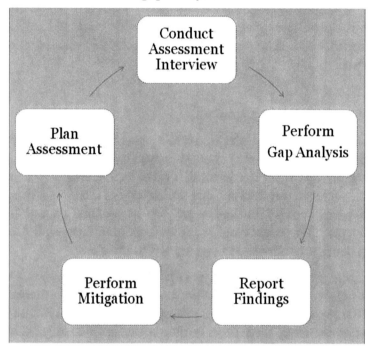

Figure 9: Risk assessment

A risk assessment is a vendor-neutral method of asking questions regarding the controls that are in place to reduce the risk of a negative outcome disrupting future operations. These are also called mitigating controls.

Controls are detective or preventive. A preventive control to keep a burglar from stealing the TV from your home is to lock the doors. A detective control is to install and arm a burglar alarm.

A risk assessment will test the existing controls to determine if they are being followed by the organization. In the previous example, to test the "doors are locked when I am out" control, we can try your door, and if it is indeed locked, the test is successful.

Risk assessments usually take the form of questionnaires, interviews and observations. In the case of evaluating multiple Cloud vendors, you might ask each of them the same series of questions. The answers can be used to rank vendors and eliminate those with the weakest controls:

- Does the Cloud provider perform their backups regularly?

- Does the Cloud provider perform background checks on its employees?

- Are adequate safety and security policies in place and, more importantly, are these followed?

- What is the outcome if the provider goes out of business?

- Do you have a plan for shifting to another source? (This brings up the business continuity and continuity of government idea again)

- Has the plan for shifting ever been tested? If so, what were the results?

Most organizations that provide these services will try to preemptively eliminate the need to respond to these typical questions over and over again. One method used is to send the same report out to all questionnaires.

Usually referred to by its regulatory name, the SAS 70 report will report on the organization's basic controls to provide a bit of assurance that they know what they are doing. There are some other more rigorous methodologies as well. Depending on what you are outsourcing, you may want to insist upon one of these for all candidates.

There is no guarantee that the provider will share their SAS 70 report. After all, the report covers security controls. It could serve as a road map for a malicious actor to attack their network.

A gap analysis is an interpretation of the risk assessment from the standpoint of reporting missing or weak controls. A gap might be that the system is only backed up once per week. So an assessment asks the questions and a gap analysis interprets the results as in the following example.

Risk assessment question: How often is client information backed up to portable electronic media and moved off-site?

"Our service employs the latest RAID technology to ensure that no single point of failure exists in our data storage network. The data storage network is backed up to magnetic tape once a week."

Gap analysis: "Our corporate policy for business continuity requires that any official corporate information stored electronically must be backed up within 24 hours of being written. If we use this vendor's system, we will be in violation of this policy unless the provider amends their backup schedule to match our minimum requirements."

Certifications - *caveat emptor*, let the buyer beware!

Statement on Auditing Standards No. 70: Service Organizations – or SAS 70 report – documents IT governance controls and provides third-party assurance of controls. The SAS 70 certification's original purpose was as a standardized method to provide service bureau customers with one single report of the accounting and logical controls used by the service provider to protect outsourced data and processes. It may document backup strategies, disaster recovery plans, human resource controls and other physical and logical controls. As we stated before, these may not be accessible without prior negotiations and mutual non-disclosure agreements.

ISO27001 documents security management and indicates a high degree of process control and commitment to information security management. The companion to ISO27001 is ISO27002, which delineates hundreds of security controls for securing the enterprise. An organization voluntarily aligns with ISO27001 and through an iterative approach of coaching and audit, will ensure these controls are in place and operating effectively.

Once they have achieved the level of alignment required for certification, they will request an independent third-party assessment of compliance. Achieving compliance with no major nonconformities, the organization may be certified by the ISO auditor, and formal application of certification by the ISO standards organization indicates that an organization has achieve a high degree of conformance with the ISO27001 standard. This certification has requirements for periodic reassessments to insure ongoing compliance.

US government systems have to comply with the Federal Information Systems Management Act or FISMA (pronounced Fiz-Ma). FISMA requires adherence to the controls specified by the National Institute of Science and Technology. Security documentation is concentrated in the 800 series of special publications. Some of the most pertinent are in the Recommended Security Controls for

Federal Information Systems and Organizations (*Errata as of 09-14-2009*).

The general roadmap for FISMA compliance dictate that the information system pass a certification process to determine, the risk(value) of the information being stored and whether adequate controls are in place to adequately protect the information. Once the system passes this audit, the system owner will receive an authority to operate from the federal agency's security office.

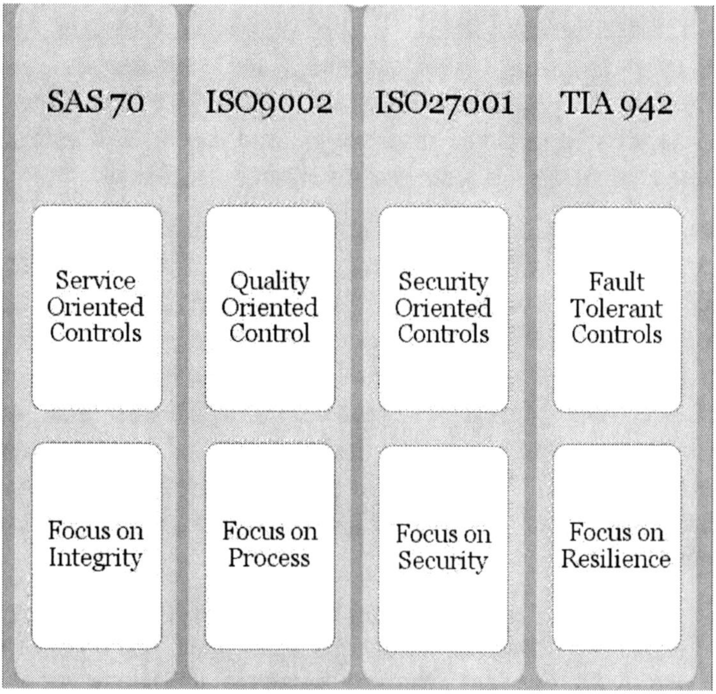

SAS 70	ISO9002	ISO27001	TIA 942
Service Oriented Controls	Quality Oriented Control	Security Oriented Controls	Fault Tolerant Controls
Focus on Integrity	Focus on Process	Focus on Security	Focus on Resilience

Figure 10: Third-party assessments

Regardless of whether the organization is required to comply with FISMA, Sarbanes-Oxley, TIA or ISO27001, the controls and goals remain the same, maintain confidentiality, integrity and availability of the information system.

Data center certification

Another widely used set of criteria are the TIA-942 data center standards issued by the Telecommunications Industry Association, which specify levels of redundancy for power, cooling and physical and logical controls. Building to the standard is not required, so this represents a voluntary standard. Certifications are awarded through external audit in tiers I to IV with tier IV representing the highest level of redundancy and indicating a high degree of resilience in the service provider. This certification started in the telecommunications industry but was quickly adopted for data centers as well.

The advantage of TIA certification lies in the confirmed level of redundancy. By certifying to the highest level, the data center is communicating they have a high degree of resiliency, dual communications paths and providers, multiple sources of power and backup systems upon backup systems. Simpler still is making sure that they are using two physical facilities to achieve some of this redundancy. Otherwise, a regional catastrophe can take out all of the above precautions with a single untoward event.

Certainty

By meeting or exceeding these certifications, the service provider has submitted to some degree of external review. This raises the likelihood that the organization is mature and has the capacity to do the job right.

The certification is a reflection of adherence to some standard or quality framework. These should not substitute due diligence on the part of the buyer.

Measuring service levels

Adequate service is defined as the minimum acceptable standard of service for the client or end-user. The service levels in IT generally follow a continuum from batch processing that can take place over a period of weeks, to real time, where the response is measured in milliseconds.

A Microsoft$^®$ Exchange or WebMail service does most of its processing in the background. Since the e-mail doesn't show up until it is processed, this can take several minutes in practice to move from the sender, through its Internet service provider (ISP), through various intermediate gateways and finally to the end ISP and the user's inbox. Since the end-user doesn't know when an e-mail has been sent, there is no expectation of how long it will take to receive, and no perception of late or early, just arrival.

The service level agreement codifies what level of service the provider will provide under the terms of the contract. This is no more complicated than standard outsourcing agreements except it may be difficult to measure and enforce the service level agreement without some clear guidelines.

The biggest issues revolve around how to measure quality of service, what sorts of service levels to expect, penalties for non-performance, what expectations for privacy and data ownerships, and what happens to residual data upon dissolution of Cloud storage and/or dissolution of the agreement.

Your side of the agreement will be all about what you will and what you won't do, such as:

- What jurisdiction any disputes will be settled in;
- Arbitration clause limiting the scope of lawsuits;
- Limits on loss to the total revenue of the contract;
- Limits on the scope of service;
- Prohibition from assuming the use of the service to provide anything that resembles critical care, life support, mission-critical support or emergency capabilities. These are strictly an assumption of risk by the client.

If you are the client, be aware that the agreement will probably stipulate these limitations. Again, go back to what is the worst that could happen. Assume that the provider fails in all provisions and your information winds up off-continent, unreachable and at ransom by the service provider in a service provider dispute. Just because the service provider is located here today doesn't mean that they could not be sucked up into a global conglomerate tomorrow. So ... you may want to include a few provisions of your own, such as:

- Change of ownership exit clause;
- Geographic limitations of data storage;
- Termination for cause;
- Handling of residual data.

Latency

Latency is the measure of the time it takes for a packet to make a round trip from point A to point B. This is useful for determining the health of the network. A network dashboard can measure latency automatically from the central hub to all of the points of interest to the organization.

Transit latency is the time it takes to travel from the user to the Cloud. Breaking response time into segments such as transit is useful in discussing service levels and measuring the current state of response *versus* tested response in the Cloud environment.

User expectations and response time

On an interactive website, the user submits a form and expects nearly instantaneous feedback. Some editing of the content can be performed locally with instant feedback, but database lookups and validations like state and zip code may have to be performed by a remote lookup.

This adds time for security validation, checksum and certificate validation. In addition, transit time across the Internet or intranet adds to the overall task length.

Finally, the overall processing can also take a toll, especially if the web server, the application server, and the database server are busy or underpowered. Adding up all the components can result in an estimated processing time per transaction. If this takes more time than the users are used to or can tolerate, fixing it after the fact may be expensive.

If the application falls into the latter category, the risks will be higher, the tolerance for failure will be lower and the cost to fix some unanticipated cyber supply-chain component may be very expensive.

Within the overall project, this type of fact gathering fits into the risk assessment stage of gaining stakeholder acceptance. By providing a realistic, even pessimistic, project plan from the outset, you can a) possibly contribute to project cancellation, b) expand the project funding to a level appropriate to the risk of failure due to hardware and software, or c) provide documentation that the issue was communicated to stakeholders who accepted it as a risk.

Culture of compliance

A key success factor for any company is when they choose to cross the border of "doing things because we have to", to adopting it "because that's who we are". "Expect the best and you may often get it," to quote Somerset Maugham. Similarly, when the security and customer service frameworks cease to be frameworks and start to become part of the organizational DNA, you can have assurance that the organization, at least, has the organization's best interests at heart.

Culture is difficult to fake, it is expensive to change, and like a plane that has reached cruising altitude, it will take less energy over time than the fits and starts of reactive security, only waking up upon impending inspection or annual audit.

Exercise versus audit

An audit is usually painful and adversarial. As the saying goes, "life outside civilized society is nasty, brutish and short". Audits typically bring out the worst and most defensive reactions. They play an important role, however, because without external review, organizations can become complacent. But because of the adversarial nature, they do not glean enough information to really improve upon current practices.

For true improvements, consider adopting training exercises. Long employed in the military and in emergency management, this technique brings up strengths and weaknesses similar to audits, but the focus is on the process, not the people. "You failed to close the gate so the sheep got out" *versus* "The sheep got out during the exercise, so how can we improve this process so they won't get out next time?"

The exercise can turn up the same weaknesses, but the latter statement is much gentler in tone. The lack of attribution lowers the risk for speaking up, and this hopefully will bring up more creative ways to start continuously improving the process.

Another benefit of exercises, particularly in environments that are large and complex, is the focus on assumptions that may or may not be true. For example, at one organization, a daily backup routine was run every day. However, when push came to shove, the process for restoring the data sets had never been created, much less tested. During an actual event, the return to service took much longer than expected.

To put this into perspective, Cloud Computing is relatively new, based on amalgams of technology with moving pieces that may not fit together as well as expected. Complex data streams may be hitting the Cloud at asynchronous times, the result being the rollback of the Cloud to some earlier state based on tape or other duplication, which may be difficult to achieve in practice.

External audit

As has become clear from observing cases such as MCI, Enron, and more recently the global financial turmoil surrounding sub-prime mortgages, there have been ever-increasing requirements for external review. In an IT organization, normally some review of internal processes takes place once or twice per year in order to comply with these financial reporting requirements.

In the United States, the Sarbanes-Oxley act required significant reporting and process review for all publicly traded corporations exceeding US$75M in annual revenue.

If the Cloud environment is hosted within the organization, the normal reporting controls may be sufficient and a more formal external review may not be mandatory.

However, there is one factor to consider that should drive even internally hosted Clouds to perform an external review, even if it is not required. There is an inherent conflict of interest introduced if the reporting is done by the same group that could be negatively affected if a bad report comes out.

Stories abound about websites with glaring security vulnerabilities that continue to exist months after they have been reported. The Cloud hosting environment will likely not be exempt.

Another non-threatening way to introduce changes in procedure is to involve the business continuity staff early on. Assuming there is someone around who is performing this function, their job is to think the gloomy thoughts, imagine the worst and hopefully set up an annual test of some sort that verifies that the Cloud is being backed up properly because they were able to recreate it at the Cloud across the way.

Early adoption techniques

When you send an e-mail, it is typically not encrypted; it joins a vast stream of other e-mails, web queries and responses, satellite office-encryption sessions and the other flotsam and jetsam of modern Internet protocol to get to the organization's e-mail server. From there, the e-mail server will bunch it all up and forward it to the remote e-mail server. Taken together, the remote server is likely connected to your server by a series of direct connections, up to 15 or more between one Internet provider and another.

The good news is this traffic seems to get from point A to point B in the blink of an eye. The bad news is that there are 15 to 20 spots between here and there that could monitor and read your e-mail, either by sorting all of the packets out and reassembling them or, if they have administrative privileges on the remote e-mail server, by reading the e-mail or replacing the e-mail target with a distribution list. It is not particularly easy, but it can be done.

The aggregate effect of exporting your e-mail hosting to a shared service provider may not represent any incremental risk to that of using an in-house provider. There actually may be a benefit since the internal IT staff may be more tempted to dip into the pool and read internal traffic than a disinterested third party.

Truly sensitive traffic should be encrypted. Several desktop encryption packages will encrypt prior to sending if the e-mail client is sure the receiver can decrypt it. Pretty Good Privacy (PGP), for example, supports a central repository of encryption keys. If the sender and the receiver's keys are both found in the repository, the e-mail is encrypted. If not, it goes through as normal. This may provide the additional layer of assurance required to reduce the risk of outsourcing e-mail to the Cloud.

This is also the case in transactional systems such as payroll. By outsourcing this function to any kind of third party, access to the info would be controlled through a rigid hierarchy with only a minimum of internal organizational gatekeepers with access. The most damage from leaking payroll information, (outside any personally identifiable bits like tax id), is likely from one co-worker to another, not to a neutral third party.

Air-gapping networks

The technique of air gapping comes up frequently in the study of control systems security. A power-plant operator has control systems software that maintains the output of the generator, controls what generators are online and what transmission lines are used, and can shut down links to any of the resources and consumers in real time. Consequently, in order to reduce the risk that someone or some process from outside the control systems environment causes one of these to occur either through maliciousness or neglect, best practice calls for a gap between the Internet, corporate systems and the control systems LAN.

Consider using similar gaps between the Internet and the Cloud environment. In order to drop content into the Cloud, instead of using a web-based connection, substitute a dedicated line using frame relay, ATM or municipal Ethernet. This reduces the attack surface for vital transactions and the risk that the Cloud updates can be disrupted using DoS or DDoS attacks.

Private Clouds

To carry this further, a private Cloud can use the same techniques to provide a dedicated access point to the Cloud as an intranet. Using more than one form of identification such as something you know and something you have is called two-factor authentication. A common example of this is the ATM card used at your bank; you have the card and you know the pin. These two together grant you access to your account.

Proper security protocols, such as separately distributed two-factor authentication using crypto key fobs like the RSA®SecurID®, Entrust® IdentityGuard or VeriSign® Tokens, generate a new pin code every minute or so. This type of technology can be used to strictly control the number of users with access to the Cloud.

Across an organization, there may be several data centers or areas ripe for consolidation. These may prove to be fertile ground for a private Cloud environment. In the case of public-sector legacy systems, there may be natural peak demand curves that offset each other. In global multinationals, this could also be the case; however, the further the processing is away from the user, the more lag time is involved in the actual transport between one site and another. Try *www.google.com* versus *www.google.co.uk* for an example.

Consider maintaining separate sites to bake fault-tolerant computing into the design. If one site or data/telecom network drops, the other site can serve as a failover.

Consider private Clouds if the information is so valuable, sensitive or dangerous that extra precautions are in order. Once data is stored in a public Cloud, you may not have as much control over who sees it, how often it is backed up, and what precautions the vendor is taking to maintain 100% availability. The vendor may be taking these precautions, but may be reluctant to share with anyone who asks simply as a like to know *versus* a need to know.

The only guaranteed method to retain control is to keep it inside the organization. One can try to enforce this requirement with an outside provider through contractual language, but if it is really that important, a contract will probably not gain the level of trust required.

Service providers should consider proactively providing proof that the data owner's information is safe, backed up, and always available in order to gain the trust and long-time patronage of these clients.

Human resources and background checks

Consider the degree of care over your own HR function mandating background checks and other surveillance. If the company has outsourced this function to a shared service provider, one can ask for it contractually, but in practice you may not have enough legal grounds to access all of the information required to insure it was done properly.

In the USA, this issue has most recently arisen in cases where the US government is considering third-party Cloud services. Some assurances are starting to surface in the press for "cleared employees only" and geographic fences for Cloud storage on government accounts. This is a relatively new area, so stay tuned.

Infrastructure

If your organization is an SMB, consider what running a 7/24/365 data center with redundant Internet pipes, hot-site failover or off-site real-time replication, 24/7 security watch centers and dual-fuel generators backing an inline UPS for a tier IV data center would cost. This sort of fault-tolerant, fully staffed redundancy doesn't come cheap. But if you have already acquired the four walls, ceiling and floor, hired the staff, built the generators/UPS combo, and linked up the multiple failover data circuits for one organization, forming a Cloud hosting company could stretch the same operating costs over multiple companies.

Multi-tenancy

Multi-tenancy means that multiple groups, departments, agencies or companies share the same space and share the costs of keeping the lights on, or the cost of keeping the Cloud hosting center floating along.

A data center normally consists of the following silos:

- Environment and facilities management
- Hardware and software management

- Network operations management
- Sales and marketing team.

This can be a mix of full-time employees and contracted staff or they can all work for the same company.

SAS 70, ISO27002 and ISO9002 all require formal policies and procedures to be established and followed. This would include the normal gates and guards on physical security as well as process controls on who has access to what, and when and how it is monitored.

The strengths of these controls should be in proportion to the value of the data. The more valuable the data or, conversely, the more damage a data loss could cause, the more you should proportionally increase the amount spent to defend it.

In the public-sector security world, this fits into the section of federated information management called system categorization. Low value and threat have corresponding low controls, medium have corresponding medium controls and high value requires correspondingly high controls. In practice, the value of the system is sometimes a judgment call. At other times, it is very clear that the cost of a loss or network penetration can be quite dear.

No matter who is managing the data center, the following questions need to be asked:

- Are staff following security best practices?
- Are there adequate HR controls in hiring and training?
- Do the staff only have access to what they need to perform their duties?

(In providing some sample questions, there are also standards in development that specifically apply to Cloud

Computing. The standards development is trailing implementations but should provide some bedrock for policies, processes and procedures in the coming years.)

This is where the value of certifications and third-party review reduce the risk that the Cloud can be punctured from within.

Avoiding miscommunication with the service provider

The business case for outsourcing is based upon cost benefit. The more complicated the process or organization being outsourced, the greater the risk that the shared service provider will do no better or actually cause some harm to the organization. Conversely, the greater the complexity, the heavier the burden on the data owner to fully communicate expectations to the service provider.

Careful selection of an outsourcing partner or selection of the largest of the available providers has been the *de facto* route to success, or at least perceived as using due diligence. But as the saying goes, if the process is screwed up and you automate it, you will have a fast, screwed-up process.

Similarly, if your organization does not have the best program or project manager, by outsourcing something the organization may not completely understand, the risk that the organization may not be understood or that the resulting process will not be understood is greater.

Assuming that the shared service provider is all-knowing, psychic or just quick enough on their feet to pull the rabbit out of the hat may put the entire organization at risk. The temptation to completely outsource some function based upon rosy financial prospects alone may be extremely short-sighted and rash.

Build understanding before you start

There are complex interconnections involved in almost any computing environment. An e-mail/WebMail system is fairly stand-alone and could theoretically function outside the confines of the organization with the exception of the access/authentication function. Usually, users want to sign on once in a network and get access to all of their resources without having to sign on again. This is called single sign on.

But what happens to single sign on when one piece of the network (e-mail) is broken off and moved to the Cloud? The answer is that single sign on stops working.

This problem can be solved by creating a link between the Cloud service provider and the enterprise network to pass sign-on requests back and forth. This solves the problem but may have created a new one. Can someone now take advantage of this to link to do something unexpected? Perhaps, but my main point is that there are usually lots of unanticipated consequences when one piece of a system is broken off and selected for outsourcing.

So far, the complexity is on the low end of the scale. The next level up could be identified as some sort of transaction server, web application or otherwise. Since the application may have to have access to enterprise databases and possibly the authentication process as well, each step to move something outside may inadvertently drag other pieces along with it, so it pays to be concerned with understanding the whole picture and not get caught up focusing only on the parts.

Communicating your needs

In order to communicate this to your shared service provider, what would you ask them to do?

- Provide the hosting service.
- Maintain adequate controls over the internal security.
- Maintain the operating environment and apply all required system patches within X days of release and Y days of testing on a similar system.
- Provide annual and periodic testing of the environment to document that controls are being followed.

Push this out to the shared service providers in the form of a request for a bid or request for information.

Gather the information, and then use project management techniques to analyze and select the best vendor.

Maintain a firm project management presence inside the organization to manage the program management office.

Remember, responsibility for the system is something that cannot be outsourced.

Agreeing on service levels: the legal frameworks for Cloud Computing

Obvious issues arise in terms of Cloud agreements. Organizations with significant investments need someone with experience in crafting outsourcing agreements.

Key terms will be price, services provided and length of contract. What is most important is, to borrow a military term, the exit strategy. If you find that the hosting provider is not adequate but you have already committed to them, especially in private Clouds where the service provider has had to perform significant work, you may have to pay a residual payment for the term of the contract. If there is a significant breech in terms of service, it may be difficult to prove fault.

Care in terms of whether this is a test environment *versus* a full implementation may drive other considerations. How committed the organization is to the vendor and how committed the vendor is to the organization are still open questions.

If the term is relatively short, the vendor's commitment will be correspondingly low; too long, and the vendor may have too much control over the agreement. If the organization cannot scale or quickly solve performance issues … well the world is full of failed attempts, but the common issue for all involved is do we want this on our watch?

The answer is, of course, no. Therefore, it is prudent to tread lightly into these agreements. It may be beneficial to set up a production test to limit the scope, set performance benchmarks and generally test the waters. It may be possible to set up several of these assessments simultaneously or in close succession in order to gauge the performance of competing vendors.

Reduce the risk by converting only new applications

In some cases, where the actual Cloud application has never been in production, this may not pose as much risk.

However, if this is a production environment, rigorous testing, controls and a disaster recovery/fallback plan are in order.

These are concerns that can be codified in a contract. However, it may be best to proceed cautiously enough through testing so that only month-to-month commitments are required. If the Cloud vendor is sufficiently large and experienced, provisioning test beds should not be an issue. If they cannot provide this, for whatever reason, it may be prudent to seek your shared service provider elsewhere.

Have an exit strategy

Termination of Cloud agreements also brings up interesting issues. Suppose you have stored some research and development off-site in Cloud storage for backup purposes. Now you have terminated the agreement. How do you ensure that all of the residual data is cleared from the Cloud storage?

If the data was stored on shared devices, will all of the backup tapes have to be destroyed? What about the data in disk storage? If it is erased, can it be recovered?

In an owned environment, you can destroy the physical devices or at least reformat the drives. In a Cloud environment, you may not even know what the physical device is, much less where it is located. This may be a very compelling issue if the information is sufficiently sensitive.

One size does not fit all

Another issue is that although two Cloud providers provide similar services, their approach and interfaces are not alike.

So it may not be as simple as switching from one Cloud to the next. There is a new standard in the offing that is recommending an open-source approach to Cloud interfaces, but this is in its early days yet so we expect at least some configuration issues when moving from one provider to another.

People again

Getting back to core competencies, the managing and provisioning of a Cloud environment requires massive attention to start up. Considerations should be given towards the existing capacity of staff, their training, whether they have passed particular certifications, and whether they have the requisite experience to set up the initial Cloud environment.

If you are entrusting your valuable organization functions and data to a third party, you had better be prepared to vet the process by which this organization staffs its data centers. This includes who they hire, and how they vet their hires.

Who has access to the data center?

Are there people with access that you wouldn't like to have access?

The level of detail may need to increase along with the value of what is at risk. At issue is who works for the service provider.

If the service provider does not provide a list, how can your organization be sure their admin is not going to sell your info?

In 2009, San Francisco, one of the largest cities in the USA, had a network admin hold their network hostage for several days by changing all of the network passwords. Only after a face-to-face impassioned appeal from the city's mayor did the culprit surrender the network passwords.

Later research determined that the admin was a convicted felon and would not have been hired had the city known his background.

What controls does the service provider have in place?

- What HR controls are in place to perform background checks and otherwise vet positions of trust?
- What security training is provided to employees?
- Is there a learning management system in place with role-based training in security and other operational procedures appropriate to the level of trust and level of risk associated with the position?

Lack of training and training protocols are an early warning signal of an immature operational environment. Since a lot of Cloud providers are just now going into business, it is incumbent upon the buyer to make sure the provider has the appropriate controls in place.

Learning management systems

A learning management system (LMS) provides role-based online security and technical training for staff. One nice thing about LMS systems is the administrator can set up courses geared towards job functions, and bundle the courses together into a mandatory curriculum based on employee job responsibilities. Then the system monitors the employees as they take and complete the course assignments. This makes it quite easy for the organization to track compliance and maintain assurance that the staff are adequately trained and aware of company policy.

We cannot overstate the value that role-based security training can provide. Simple concepts such as, "if you see something, say something" and "challenge anyone who is not badged or is unknown to you in your work area" can provide lingering dividends.

Training to maintain physical control can prevent a malicious actor from installing monitoring or other devices in the data center. If you have something of value in your network, it is likely that someone would go to these lengths to steal it.

The use of LMSs would indicate a level of maturity in the organization's approach to training. This is one method that can be used to reduce vulnerabilities in multiple areas.

Company security policies

- Do they have them?
- Does everyone know what they are?
- Are they followed to the letter as well as in spirit?

The security policies can be plastered everywhere but if the employees don't understand them or haven't been properly trained in physical and logical security protocols, especially in a public Cloud environment since it is likely to have some sort of Internet access points, millions of individual users' information could be at risk.

Disaster recovery and business continuity planning

The same goes for business continuity planning. Even the Cloud can experience outages. On one hosting site, 100,000 websites were wiped out overnight due to a configuration problem. Google™'s Gmail has had some high-profile outages recently, as has the Microsoft® Sidekick e-mail hosting service.

- Do they have a backup and recovery plan?
- Have they tested it?
- Does a review of the latest recovery test reveal any concerns?

Even though these technologies appear too big to fail, the ultimate responsibility for protecting information lies with the user, not the host, so take appropriate precautions by questioning and testing the service provider's backup and recovery procedures. Anticipate the worst, but hope for the best.

Depth on the bench

As the Cloud vendors return requests for proposal and requests for information, some mention of how they hire and retain staff should be in order:

- How do they screen employees?
- Do they periodically rescreen?
- As they lose staff in a year, how do they bring on new talent and advance existing staff?

If they do not have adequate staffing levels, they may be willing to sacrifice service levels to your detriment, especially if they think they may have options that prevent you from rapidly finding a replacement service such as large quantities of your data stored in their data centers or proprietary technology that will require significant effort to move to another platform.

Separation of duties and need to know

Consider mandating formal controls in the service level agreement on who has access to organization data. Larger data storage organizations may be able to always execute, but because they are larger, it may be more difficult to determine who has access.

Smaller data storage organizations may be inadequately capitalized and could go out of business overnight with no contingency plan in place to salvage or transfer your data. These bleak outcomes may, in fact, occur unless you have adequate legal and financial protections in place to prevent this from happening.

Financial health of the service provider

The financial health of the service provider can have an impact on staffing, training and maintenance. They can also be influenced by merger and acquisition activity. Any fundamental changes in the service provider organization should be firewalled from the data owner. If a merger does impact the execution of the service level agreement, the exit clause should have an option that covers this contingency.

Financial risk

Capital expense and operating expense should theoretically eventually meet. Buy something and depreciate it, *versus* rent it and pay a bit more for rent *versus* buy. The unknown factor is whether the capital costs drop over time or increase. Assuming an increase, buying can save money. The downstream risk is if the product you are buying is obsolete before the end of the depreciation term, renting would be better.

The difference has been termed technological risk. If someone comes up with a better, faster way of doing things, it may be worth taking a loss on the capital expense and switching to the new method. The old legacy software app is buried and the new, cool app is born.

The trend, though, is obvious; with more and more applications available online through portals, it is only prudent to consider them as options. Outsourcing a function to a service provider transfers the risk of technology obsolescence to the provider. However, if the service provider goes out of business, the organization could experience a disruption in service. Consider adding an exercise to determine how rapidly the organization can transition to a new provider. Even if the provider is financially strong and committed today, in today's rapidly evolving landscape that may not be a guarantee for tomorrow.

CHAPTER 4: TOWER CLEARANCE

In embarking on a Cloud Computing project, it is important to assess the risks, come up with strategies to mitigate the risks and communicate any that aren't sufficiently covered.

In practical terms, this involves a mix of project management and business continuity best practices to arrive at a) the overall risk of the project, and b) what can be done to mitigate or lower the risk to acceptable levels.

Risk assessments take into account fire, flood and other intentional and unintentional disruptions caused by people. These are multiple pathways that can disrupt the people, processes and technology that drive an organization's effectiveness.

Other outside dependencies like power and light, gas and water, postal services, inbound and outbound logistics (shipping), data and telecommunications are all likely to be providing inputs and managing outputs independent of your control and oversight.

Organizational impact: what would happen if?

What would happen to the organization, customers, brand and staff if power was cut for the local area for an extended period? What would happen if diesel or natural gas delivery was disrupted? Are the generators capable of running on multiple fuels? What is the minimum workspace required to perform the most essential tasks? If the workspace was not available, what would happen?

Mitigation strategies: what can we do to lessen impact?

Mitigation strategies introduce stacking-the-deck strategies to minimize the impact of events. If you depend upon the Internet to communicate, installing a satellite link and/or a cellular data link as a backup might prevent an outage. If voice is critical, alternatives, such as voice over IP or cell over IP can provide communications in a crisis.

Continuity plans: keep going if the worst happens

A continuity plan is simply the formalization of the steps you must take to continue operations in the face of a disruption. Once the ideas start flowing on how to keep things from occurring, management will buy in to the alternate strategies and fund practicing drills for the reaction strategies that kick in after the event has occurred.

Testing the continuity plan

Most organizations start testing by requesting comments on the written plan, then move to a structured walkthrough or a group edit, then up to a tabletop exercise.

In a tabletop exercise, the players represent a particular business role, such as the accounting manager or IT manager. The exercise referee announces the type of disruption. The players then walk through in a timed round what they would do about the disruption.

The exercise helps ensure that the plan has no gaps in coverage and the staff understand the plan well enough to execute under the pressure of real events. These are exercises. There is no right or wrong answer.

Figure 11: Business continuity planning

The only wrong answer is answering no to the question "Did we test this?" when we actually have to undergo the real thing. This level of planning helps identify areas of risk and also contributes to formally devising plans to reduce the risk to an acceptable level.

External *versus* internal hosting providers

An external hosting provider will provide some economies of scale, especially if the organization is small or medium-sized. Larger entities may also benefit if the application or infrastructure is a commodity. The external provider may be able to provide additional services than are available internally at a reduced cost.

For example, e-mail and WebMail generally are favorably evaluated for conversion because a) the transactions generally traverse the Internet anyway, and b) the actual transaction processing is usually done within the confines of some narrowly defined application hosts with very little customization, or customization that can be easily duplicated by an outsourcing partner.

Exceptions may be sensitive government or civilian traffic. This may be so sensitive that the actual e-mail does not traverse public networks. In these cases, it can still be converted to a private Cloud hosting facility, provided the service provider requires rigorous HR background checks, and substantial and documented internal controls.

When your hosting provider is so strict that an organization is not authorized to visit its own hosting facility unescorted, we may be approaching the appropriate level of strictness required to outsource the most sensitive transaction processing. Even so, there are, quite frankly, some applications that may not fare well in a Cloud environment.

Information such as that with a high risk for theft or that could cause major financial loss if misused, or anything that is proprietary intellectual property or could cause risk to life or property may not be suitable to store electronically at all.

Identifying the risk of the information stored on a public or private Cloud service provider is a key issue in identifying and quantifying risk. A public Cloud is hosted on shared resources open to the public. A private Cloud hosts only information on systems dedicated to one entity.

Private Clouds

The private Cloud model uses the shared service model, but all of the customers for the Cloud are internal. The advantages are that with top management support, a modicum of shared effort and shared goals, a private Cloud running internally can be created using the same best practices and approaching the efficiency of a public Cloud service provider, without some of the security concerns of turning internal data over to third party.

If the main objective is to reduce operating costs by providing a shared platform, this may work very well. Using Cloud Computing techniques can increase the efficiency of internal operations, plus, there should be some savings from not having to maintain as vigilant a watch over the service provider, so this option may be as cost-effective as the public Cloud option while avoiding some of the stress and security concerns that apply mainly to public Cloud environments.

Public Clouds: there is an app for that

Google™ Apps, Twitter and MySpace all use a public Cloud model. The advent of the iPhone™ and the app is a great example of where the market and probably some areas of our future computing environment are going in interacting with public Clouds. If you need to map restaurants, there is an app; need a way to calculate calories consumed, there is an app for that as well; app to learn the latest guitar chords, check. The most interesting thing is that the clamor about the level of security concerns on this platform has not reached the same decibel level as with every other computing platform.

The same goes for the HP DreamScreen and Blackberry® smartphones. Since their interfaces are relatively specialized, and do not have enough of a financial or privacy surface to make them worthy targets, these apps have been relatively pain free. Once they become more ubiquitous, this may change, but in the interim, have you heard about antivirus for iPhones™ or Blackberrys®?

Similarly, with Cloud applications, it is possible to design them with such a limited interface that it becomes very difficult to launch an attack through them. This is similar to a computer virus, since once you block the receptor that the virus likes to attack, it can't replicate and moves on to another host or else just dies.

Smart services

Once in the Clouds, as more organizations adopt interoperable applications, the access to services should be unprecedented.

For example, many security providers now provide a Cloud-based security service that will redirect all of your web traffic through their security network operations, scan for attacks, and then peel off the good stuff to forward to your e-mail servers and end-users. The multilayered approach to security has been in place in large public and private institutions for many years and now is accessible as a Cloud service by small and medium-sized organizations as well.

Putting this layer in the Cloud makes sense since we are most fearful of penetration from the Internet and also, by concentrating the outermost defenses in a gigabit bandwidth front door, the amount of spurious traffic delivered to your web browser is significantly less. This cuts down on the noise in the network and should improve web response time and allow users and managers to worry about the mission, not defending against net barbarians.

Hybrid Clouds

The hybrid Cloud model takes into account that some organizations may not entrust public Cloud service providers with their most sensitive functions.

Looking at applications on a continuum, social networks and blogs would be hosted on public Clouds. Intranet collaboration sites would be hosted in third-party managed private Clouds. Finally, intellectual property and other sensitive systems are hosted within the private Cloud.

In practice, the modern enterprise is a collection of public and private database interactions so the hybrid Cloud model is not a huge step from where we are operating today.

The next steps may be baby steps or large ones, but it is likely this process will continue. Pushing onward to develop and participate, balancing the need for reduced cost, increased privacy or speed to market, allows us to have our cake and eat it too.

Client defenses

Of course, this does not guarantee net safety. The biggest threats come from visiting bad websites or opening an infected e-mail attachment. Once the desktop is infected with a virus, it is difficult to diagnose, and difficult to treat. The great perimeter defense doesn't work all the time; see the Maginot Line and Operation Overlord or ask your local cybersecurity chief if they completely trust their firewalls. If all we needed was perimeter defenses, there would be no antivirus or desktop security suites.

This sort of discussion belongs in the worst-case scenario analysis. Understanding what could happen should produce some obvious and not so obvious scenarios that I collectively call "living in the land of bad things".

Fiscal control systems may fall into this as well if the network or someone in the network has access to moving money around and it doesn't take a boatload of paperwork to do it. It may be prudent to consider using a dumb terminal with a dedicated line to the financial network to perform this sort of work.

Even EDI and XML systems are at risk with a skilled programmer and unfettered access, so there are generally accountants and technical reviews and all sorts of management oversight in place to make sure account Z balances to account Y. But pushing to move some of these management systems closer to the outside wall may bring along additional risks.

Implementing large systems or converting an existing system to the Cloud has some advantages in terms of moving from a big ticket system to a rentable, scalable, vendor-supported system. As long as the level of customization required to support your business model is there and the hosting provider can meet the same level of rigor introduced in the previous example, there are not any inherently different considerations than for the first case.

There are some security concerns in that the availability of significant amounts of personally identifiable or fiscal information on the Web may translate into a weakness.

However, the same argument can be made for storing the information in a corporate data center. Once someone has penetrated the corporate network, don't they have the same or similar access?

So one can argue the risks cancel each other out and move on to examine the other risks inherent in these types of consideration. There are some differences in the Cloud environment; nearly every component will have some sort of exposure to the Internet. This increase in the attack surface may bring vulnerabilities to the surface so care should be taken in evaluating potential risks.

With systems such as Salesforce.com, the customer relationship management system can reduce the time required to merge views from multiple systems into a globally accessible customer view. This may allow clients acquiring other companies with similar or cross-selling opportunities the ability to quickly digest the acquisition to the point of having visibility across the new global enterprise.

Similar benefits accrue for financial systems vendors that have data mapping and import tools that can read from multiple legacy data formats. The ability to see the financial picture quickly after an acquisition can provide critical situational awareness, and with the rapidly changing economic landscape, may represent a mission-critical application.

Strategies for managing change

There may be significant risk in the area of change management. That is, losing your way in the process of conversion. This can occur in any number of ways, but the most common is not getting wide-enough management support and comprehension on the front end. Also, without an experienced guide, it is easy to follow distractions and get bogged down in the mud along the way. With the velocity of change in technology today, failure to execute a project such as this without some immediate benefit or payback represents a high risk.

It may be likened to taking a wagon train across the old west, only to find the destination city had turned into a ghost town by the time you arrived.

Break the project into smaller parts for pilot projects

Before going all in, there may be some smaller, shorter, less risky projects. These build confidence and can quiet critics if done first with good results. Web-based time and attendance, expense reports and travel portals all fall into necessary evils that may lend themselves to a quick implementation.

Other options such as wikis and blogs to share knowledge come at a lower price for cost of entry to design, and probably a lower psychic toll if they don't catch on, than converting the organization's financial reporting, HR or enterprise requirements planning system into a Cloud application and getting it wrong.

Clearly specify in the project charter that this project will have multiple phases. The earliest phase will be a non-production test known as a pilot. The pilot phase will implement 50 to 70% of the project functionality in order to gauge the project's viability. This allows the project team some leeway in determining the outcomes and provides feedback for later project phases.

Progressive elaboration

By adding in a pilot phase, the overall project definition can be a bit looser in terms of definitions. This can reduce the stress on the project design team, allow for a faster start-up, and reduce overall project anxiety. If the pilot goes well, the pilot design can be amended to produce a more robust planning requirement for future iterations. This is called progressive elaboration. Other wags may refer to this as "making it up as you go along".

Regardless, it is nicely in line with what President Obama once suggested with "do not make the perfect, the enemy of the good". By starting small, with lighter requirements, the overall implementation can be launched with a P1 light version, followed by P2, P3 and P4 with progressively more complex iterations.

Testing

Testing is probably one of the most underappreciated functions in the development world. An effective rigorous testing program can sidestep many of the known vulnerabilities that, if left unaddressed, tend to land organizations and their Internet development team in the unwanted spotlight.

Examples may include SQL injection vulnerabilities, unencrypted data and applications traffic, any and all of which can be used by the garden-variety script kiddy to take down your website, steal information or credentials, and implant malicious code to perform even more nasty tricks down the road, at their leisure.

Use case testing

Use cases are short descriptions of a typical transaction that would be performed by a user of the application. The use case could read, "allow user to enter, update or cancel a transaction".

Test scripts

These are the scripts that a tester follows to test a particular use case. A test script may have multiple paths to get to the appropriate answer.

In testing the ability of a user to cancel transactions, test scripts are written for every likely scenario: user cancels prior to billing, user cancels while transaction is in transit, user cancels after billing, user attempts to cancel canceled transaction, etc.

The test scripts developed from this can be followed by a tester and the quality of the deliverable can be measured based on the outcomes.

Tabletop testing

This testing takes the use cases, the test scripts, some knowledgeable users and walks through each script manually. The tabletop is useful for validating the use cases and the test scripts.

Since the typical end-user probably does not realize the significance of use cases and test scripts, you may couch the meeting as an informal review of the application design.

Consider adding tests around concepts like: the application hosting environment will be tested by a security auditor using software such as Nessus or Metasploit and reveal no major vulnerabilities. Any major vulnerabilities found will be reviewed by the security provider and the organization. Any vulnerabilities that are mutually agreed to be the responsibility of the service provider must be corrected by the service provider within four weeks. Failure to correct such vulnerabilities within the four-week period constitutes a breech of contract.

Automating these types of review and making them mandatory will reduce the risk that the application or hosting environment will reach pilot or production level with significant flaws. It demonstrates a degree of care that should inspire like-minded thinking on the part of the project team to stop the production line if a significant problem is discovered.

Documentation of testing

Documentation can be a manual or automated log. Depending on the degree of complexity, there may be performance and capacity testing on the platform as well.

If the users test the system and it is sluggish during optimum conditions, it will only be worse in production.

Capacity or performance testing can help smooth out unexpected problems. A system that works perfectly, but is too slow to use, will not last the week.

Automated testing can often generate documentation of test completions. This is also useful if the system is stable and only an incremental change needs to be tested. By comparing the results with previous steady-state tests, the end-user can have some assurance of the impact of changes on the system.

These examples are meant as a primer on the subject of testing. In practice, a full-blown system will need a rigorous test plan. Another useful test is for the export of data. If we know that the source environment is at state X (2,150,003,128) database records, the target-system database record count must be the same. By tasking out the formal comparison of one system to the next, it may be possible to avoid database integrity problems that may be impossible to correct if the starting conditions are not captured.

Database integrity problems for one organization cost 9 months and US$900,000 to correct. Still, in the overall scheme of things, even this is a relatively light loss compared with the cost of credit monitoring, US$30 to US$50 per leaked record. The cost and the corresponding risk of loss are high if the organization is handing off personally identifiable information to either the hosting database, or conceivably any of the contributing databases to the hosting environment.

Risk of loss versus testing costs

If the risk of loss is large, the testing should be correspondingly vigorous. Conversely, looking forward to lower-risk pilots, it may not be necessary to test every scenario.

Alternate testing strategies can reduce the cost of testing. Making the vendor responsible for some testing, leveraging internal controls testing with other external testing, and asking end-users to voluntarily participate as subject-matter experts can reduce the cost.

4: Tower Clearance

Certification of data centers

Using the concept of certification does not completely cover the application testing environment. Since the application is a symbiotic entity on top of the Cloud infrastructure, it will no doubt change the infrastructure in ways that may be difficult to predict. Therefore, one cannot substitute certification.

One can, however, use certification as an attestation that some things are in place like employee screening, user authentication mechanisms, and employee and user life-cycle provisioning to remove users if they depart or no longer need access.

Tier III and tier IV certification refer to fault tolerance. They may cover some of the basics on availability. To be clear, security concerns are incalculable without any context. For example, famous secret recipes have value far beyond the printed words on paper. Similarly, other intellectual property, trade secrets, sensitive personal information such as client lists, personal information, health data, financial data, and transactional controls may all be at risk if they are stored anywhere on your network, much less on an externally hosted site.

So the calculus becomes faster, better, cheaper *versus* private, private, private! This is not a deal breaker for Cloud Computing. It is a warning to get the bits right that really matter. The cost of fixing a breech, if it can be fixed, will far outweigh the costs of due diligence, proper legal review and possibly scheduling face-to-face service-provider interviews to validate all the hype and marketing material telling you how well the vendor will take care of your data.

Pick on the little guy

If there is a smaller part of the organization that may be a bit more nimble, is willing to trade pain for the gain of accessing the latest and greatest ... and at the same time not as integrated, they may be a target candidate to push out the global system. Once they have taken some of the hard knocks, the rest of the organization can be slowly converted to their system. This may be worth a look to do the same, even if the smaller group is integrated.

Continuity of operations planning

Using continuity of operations planning techniques can help organize the dialogue of what are the advantages and disadvantages of the various paths to the Cloud, and if there are some hybrid scenarios to consider as well.

If one part of the organization is in the Cloud, either through first adopters' strategies or through acquisition, the information must flow freely and securely from one system to another. Manual systems and poorly controlled batch interfaces (called two-tier or n-tier computing) generally add levels of risk at the interface level.

What happens if a transaction or a bunch of transactions get lost? The controls must be in place to monitor all the systems involved and ensure that at the end of the day, all of them reflect the same view of the world. There is not any inherently different level of risk on the Cloud *versus* the n-tier computing model. The risk is only aggravated by the use of the Internet channel as a method of transport.

This can be mitigated in part through the use of VPN connections. However, there are some other moving parts here that should be discussed as well.

Protecting data with encryption

Since your organization information is on shared storage, it would be helpful to prevent any backup tapes from being read by a casual employee if they gain access or if backup tapes are lost or stolen. The most common control to prevent this is to encrypt the data as it is written to disk. In terms of performance, unless the encryption is baked into the storage hardware, the information stored on the Cloud is unlikely to be encrypted.

Unencrypted data protection

Once copied to the Cloud, what happens to unencrypted data when it is erased? In the physical realm, data does not actually disappear; it is still resident on the physical data drives. The link to the data that allows you to access it is broken. A sophisticated IT person can reestablish the link and read the information if they have the requisite access rights to the physical device.

This is the same sort of thing that is performed by software packages, such as the Norton™ Undelete command on PCs. The counter is to use programs such as the PGP FIPS delete command to write several routes of zeros and ones across an erased file to prevent anyone from reading deleted material.

Data loss prevention

Data loss prevention software monitors the stored data by keyword or explicitly to track sensitive files.

The only way to secure these environments with any degree of certainty is to disconnect the data storage from the

Internet and restrict all browser, e-mail and removable media/USB drive capability from the clients hooked up to the limited-access network.

Once a Cloud environment goes global, the privacy issues multiply. The jurisdiction for Cloud data and the circumstances under which it can be disclosed vary widely. Some transactions may not be protected at all if they originate in the USA and are transported internationally (Patriot Act). Designing the controls for the service may require discovering under what circumstances items can be disclosed, what will be encrypted and who can decrypt.

If a preannouncement of a corporate financial statement is stored on the Cloud, the goals of a data-loss prevention system would be to:

- Restrict access to the document;
- Produce an audit trail showing if the document is read and by whom;
- Restrict the distribution of the document.

Data loss prevention software is designed to do just that, but this is new technology and should only be relied upon as one control among many designed to keep the right bits safe.

Stay in touch with the Cloud!

If you use the Internet to connect back-end databases to the Cloud database, the connection must be resilient. By this I mean that if it is really important to the process that the connection from the enterprise to the Cloud be resilient and always on, then pay for the most reliable, dedicated, redundant private circuit using some kind of transport other than Internet-based VPNs.

This is to maintain the circuit in the face of DDoS attacks and to prevent the traffic from being intercepted through the various Internet routing points that could be sampled by a malicious actor.

This may be even more critical if you are sharing network security tables and password hashes to maintain single sign-on services in the Cloud. Password hashes is a method used to encrypt and store passwords so they can't be read. Unfortunately, hackers can sometimes use the hashes to guess or even substitute the encrypted version to gain access to restricted systems.

People, process, and then technology

And finally, one of the most important issues is people. It has been said many times that security is not a technical problem, it is a people problem. People at the managed service level are not directly in your control. The process and maybe a bit of the technology are the only things one can directly influence.

In terms of HR controls, because the Cloud provider will have access to your data, it is important that you have a level of comfort that they are performing background checks before hiring personnel, that these personnel are well trained for the duties assigned and that processes and procedures are in place to maintain these standards of conduct.

In the Cloud environment, the infrastructure behind the Cloud is complex and massively expensive to duplicate.

There are incentives to just get by with just enough resources to serve today, plus a bit more.

Consider spreading the Cloud environment amongst several vendors to compensate for this lack of visibility. However, by dropping the single vendor concept, you may be buying further trouble by managing two separate organizations.

Like the two pieces of metal that tell you which one is coldest, the two vendors will tell you that one is better in some areas while the other might serve pages faster. The real tests come when the chips are down. Splitting the workload may in fact be prudent, but it may overtax internal resources to monitor performance.

The strength of third-party auditors in certifying Cloud vendors is:

- They audit multiple companies.
- They tend to get better at this over time.
- They will provide some punch that is difficult to argue with *versus* your opinion alone.
- They are not responsible for the negative outcomes of the audit.

Trial and error is probably not the best choice of audit techniques either; nor is flying blind. Early on, prior to signing anything, ask for references:

- Check the references; see what problems and techniques they used in selecting a vendor.
- Check the vendor's financial health. Financial problems can lead down the path of dropped maintenance and deferred patches, and can put off major software infrastructure upgrades even though the new coolness is much more secure than the old lameness.

This is one reason why certifications like ISO9002, TIA-942 and ISO27001 for managed service providers are so important. They are indications of not only talking the talk and walking the walk, but striving to maintain a culture of compliance. The culture of compliance states that staff will do what's right not because they have to, nor because they get in trouble if they do not; it is because they want to provide this level of service.

Certifications matter

The higher the bar for certification, the less likely you will get one of those 3 am phone calls. This is one of the reasons, that TIA, ISO9002 and ISO27001 certifications mean so much in the outsourcing arena. A simple SAS 70 report is a snapshot, made once per year to address concerns primarily made from an accounting standpoint.

ISO9002 certification is quality driven and may not talk as much about service performance as one would like. It is possible to exclude items from the scope of certification if they do not impact the quality of the service provided. This gives the service provider a lot of leeway on what should or should not be covered by the scope of the certification.

ISO27001 is suitably different in this regard. Driven by the International Standards Organization, testing requirements and certification requirements are quite stringent. For any service organization seeking this accreditation, the requirements are as follows:

1 Mentoring
2 Certification
3 Auditing
4 Maintenance
5 Reauditing every year.

This is not about quality alone. The organization must pass cultural and performance testing as well.

Procedural documentation requirements are similar to ISO9002 service organization quality controls. Documented procedures for testing, calibrating test equipment, procedure step-by-steps and check lists determine that the process will be in place and followed from one incident to the next.

Supplier corrective action reports (SCARs) and customer corrective action reports (CCARs) are provided as checkpoints in the process. A SCAR or CCAR can drive any number of changes in process and procedures. By following transactions that have gone wrong, reacting to them and improving the process along the way, the quality system begins to take hold and drives further advances.

Dropping back to ISO27001, the quality process takes on even more heft. The ISO27001 specification was written specifically for IT operations.

Continuity of operations, service-level agreements and help-desk functions are all supposed to follow standards. Statistics of incident tracking and resolution reduce the chance of recurrence.

These are effective in private Cloud environments. By instituting an external review of controls that is continuous, the private Cloud provider can break through the adversarial and reactive annual audit perspective to the more lasting and effective culture of compliance model.

The cost of monitoring an external organization to ensure they have implemented (and continue to implement) adequate safeguards will need to be considered at the front end.

If you can't monitor the organization yourself, you will have to rely on the organization or its external auditor to certify their controls. The more sensitive the information processing outsources, the more exceptionally strong and well documented the certification required.

Regardless of whether you are using a public or private Cloud service provider, these individuals are now virtually part of your organization and you will want them to adhere not to bronze standards, but to platinum standards.

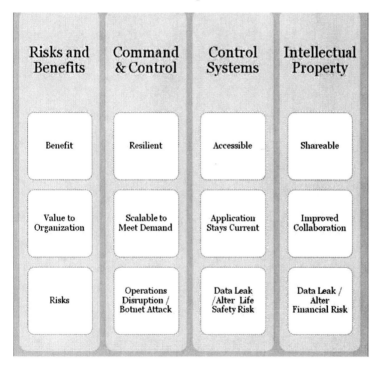

Figure 12: Cloud stop apps

In the long view, if you save a bit by going to managed services, but wind up losing your reputation because the provider mishandled it or could not provide the level of service your customers require, that's not staying above the Clouds, that's crashing through them.

CHAPTER 5: SECURING THE CABIN

There is a saying that a cart that overturns in the road ahead is a warning to the one behind. The closer the organization can stay with the mainstream of computing research, the more likely the organization will be able to benefit from someone else's overturned cart.

Conversely, every organization adopting the same systems and sharing open access among a largely unregulated and unsupervised workforce may also be vulnerable to the same attack.

A random e-mail or spam can be opened by the lowliest clerk or the highest executive. A website that appears to be only advertising the services of a fellow professional organization can be completely riddled with malware and spyware.

It would appear that driving towards Cloud Computing as the ubiquitous platform for all is imprudent. By definition, the majority of hacking attacks are directed at the mainstream. Hackers have been known to adopt lesser-known browsers for their own personal use precisely because they recognize the risk posed by using mainstream software.

Recognize the risk in order to avoid the consequences

From the individual's perspective, the risk is personal information and assets with any connection to the Internet. Visit the wrong site with the right browser settings, and an infected site installs malicious software on the desktop.

Once installed, any information can be shared and sent back to the hacker controlling the system.

This translates into a broader risk once the desktop client is infected, since it can pass this to other users. Eventually, an administrator may become infected and the entire network could be at risk.

In order to defend against this and other sorts of network attacks, the organization has to have defense in depth. Defense in depth means one can't rely on any single control to protect sensitive information; there must be multiple controls in place to reduce the risk to acceptable levels.

Defense in depth strategies

As a continuum of controls, an individual machine may have a user ID and password to prevent access. Most systems are now shipping with some type of file encryption so that if the machine is booted off an external drive or CD-ROM, the system will still not reveal any information without the proper credentials.

Further up the food chain are computer networks. Networks are protected by passwords and user ids, limiting access to files based on need. Patching regimens correct software flaws within the operating system as they are found.

PCs and servers on the network send requests to the Internet and other network segments and receive replies. These in-and-out requests are often referred to as network traffic or simply traffic. Once traffic leaves the network, it reaches the transportation segment. For example, the Internet is a transport. Frame relay, broadband cable and ISDN are also examples of network transport.

5: Securing the Cabin

The traffic may be encrypted in order to reduce the chance of someone in the middle gathering information that can be used to attack the network. Examples of encrypted traffic are VPNs and secure socket layer (SSL) encryption for browser to website connections.

Networks are often divided into internal- and external-facing segments. A PC or server machine on the Internet facing the network may not be able to see the internal configuration due to a device called a firewall. All network communications to and from the Internet converge through the firewall. The firewall is able to recognize and filter out communications that may be harmful, based on set rules.

At the far end of the spectrum are more sophisticated network protection devices called application firewalls that strictly limit the type of traffic allowed to pass. There are also devices called intrusion detection systems that look for known types of attack and send alerts. Combining some of the features of the intrusion detection system (IDS) and firewalls are intrusion prevention systems (IPSs) that not only send alerts when they detect an attack, but also block all traffic that is related to the attack.

There is also the option to deploy network access protection (NAP) devices that only let preregistered devices onto the network. Without the preregistration, the devices' access is denied or severely restricted.

All of these methods together can reduce the risk somewhat. At the high end of the scale is the network watch center. This is a fully staffed network operations center that monitors the systems for attacks and can take decisive action to limit the damage and access of attackers once they are discovered. They can also monitor passively to gather evidence for possible prosecution of an attacker.

The main point is, the better prepared the organization, the less likely the attack will be successful.

There are some new developments along these lines. The types of attack that are called DoS attacks maul sites using multiple machines. Since the attacking networks are so large, the corresponding defenses have to be large to compete. With a large Internet security provider, who has gigabits of Internet bandwidth, the attack can be dissipated and only critical scanned traffic is allowed to flow through to the organization.

This is similar in effect to having only trusted partners access the network through a private network connection. Trying to maintain this level of disconnect actually takes the network back 20 years, when the majority of networks were private. The convergence of old tech helping new is certainly ironic, but may be the way of the future as trust becomes more important than access.

Cloud security operation centers

There are a growing number of security providers that cater to the Cloud. Since the Cloud can be amorphous, the network monitoring priorities can get lost. Specifically, you must trust the company hosting the data, trust the organization or trust some third party.

Because of the nature of networks, security monitoring can actual reside anywhere. Just as a burglar alarm can be monitored remotely, security services using boxes called sensors can monitor the network traffic and report back to a central monitoring station. As long as the network is monitored 24/7, it may actually be cost-effective, and more effective, to have an external provider perform this service.

The model thus established can look at traffic from the standpoint of what is expected and report on deviations; it can go deeper and decide if the content is within the expectations; or it can look at an even deeper level to determine if certain keywords are present, and see if this content should be making its way outside of the network.

The latter type of inspection falls into the category of data loss prevention. For example, it is a bit easier for a neutral third party to question a vice-president's transfer of the balance sheet to a competitor, than for a captive IT organization to do so.

User provisioning

Since a third party has to be informed of all additions, changes and separations of staff, this may or may not be a motivator to rapidly alert all affected parties to these types of change.

In a typical organization, there may be dozens of systems that each have to have an entry for a staff member to access them. The priority is usually on granting access because a new staff member without access does not contribute much to the bottom line. A transferred or separated worker may not receive the same amount of attention. A lapse in revoking authorization in these cases can result in employee opportunities for ongoing physical and logical access to systems. If the worker is disgruntled, the damage that can be done may be without limits.

This same issue exists with the Cloud environment and may be amplified if there is not sufficient automation to tie the internal systems of control together with the external access provided by the Cloud environment.

The generic category of software used to bridge these gaps is entitled employee provisioning or employee life-cycle processing. The HR department hires, separates or notes a transfer. Behind the scenes, an alert or an actual processing event occurs that changes the access based on the type of event.

This is also called database propagation, where a change in one database that logically affects another is transmitted and applied to all subsequent databases.

It is not as important that this process be automated as much as that the process is followed. It is also fairly easy to verify that the process is being followed. Simply pull five or ten separations and transfers, go to the IT department and ask to see the corresponding security records reflecting that the changes were indeed applied.

Security and authentication in the Cloud

If the data is transmitted on the Internet or processed using a third party's system, it may be at risk. In order to protect it, adequate safeguards must be implemented. Larger organizations may have the tools and capabilities to monitor networks and Cloud implementations using existing tools. If this is the case, consider leveraging these existing controls as the first option.

If this is not the case, rather than creating a new department or relying on the vendor, consider hiring a third party to monitor the enterprise network and the Cloud-based applications. The reliance on a third party removes the possibility of a conflict of interest with the vendor and the possibility of complacency with the internal staff.

5: Securing the Cabin

If we look at the future, perhaps the Cloud will evolve into the most secure and trusted zone as opposed to bearing the slightly murky reputation it has today. By moving operations to the Cloud and only using the PC as a viewer, for example, we may be able to defuse the issues of unpatched PC clients spreading viruses and worms like Conficker. Internet service providers are already capable of detecting viruses and worms in transit. A self-diagnosing and self-cleaning Cloud can't be far behind.

CHAPTER 6: TAKE OFF

Reducing these operational risks may be enough of a motivation to at least examine the possibility of moving to Cloud Computing. The same restrictions apply. First, seek to understand your current systems. Second, look at the available options and goals for the organization. Where there are overlaps for Cloud Computing advantages, the disadvantages that may exist below the surface are likely to be security and transportation costs. If you fail to factor these into your analysis, it may turn out to be less advantageous in the short run to convert even one application to Cloud Computing.

If it's on the Internet, it belongs in the Cloud

If you have a payroll inquiry application on the Web, putting it on the Cloud may reduce the impact this application can have on your overall processing needs. It can also reduce the likelihood of a DoS attack disrupting other operations.

NASDAQ moved its historical financial reporting to the Cloud. Moving public-facing sites to the Cloud pushes the attack surface into the larger Internet, away from the organizational infrastructure. The only Internet-accessible targets are then hidden behind a corporate firewall and less likely to be disrupted.

If the transactions on the Web do not require real-time access, copy the records likely to be queried by pushing them to a Cloud-accessible database. This reduces the attack surface again, by eliminating the need for the application to be connected beyond the organization's internal network applications' firewall.

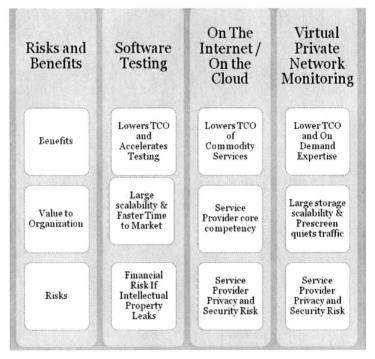

Risks and Benefits	Software Testing	On The Internet / On the Cloud	Virtual Private Network Monitoring
Benefits	Lowers TCO and Accelerates Testing	Lowers TCO of Commodity Services	Lower TCO and On Demand Expertise
Value to Organization	Large scalability & Faster Time to Market	Service Provider core competency	Large storage scalability & Prescreen quiets traffic
Risks	Financial Risk If Intellectual Property Leaks	Service Provider Privacy and Security Risk	Service Provider Privacy and Security Risk

Figure 13: Cloud go apps

E-mail in the Clouds

Moving e-mail servers to the Cloud only duplicates what Google™ and Yahoo® have done for years. Getting these applications out of the corporate network reduces the stress and workload on the local IT staff. By locating them up in the telecom infrastructure, the threat of DDoS is again reduced, assuming a massive gigabit pipe is available for the e-mail services to the Cloud.

The user authentication can reside either in the Cloud or via a secure private line back to the corporate network. This connection is hopefully lightly used and can be set up to echo security from the main organizational security servers to the remote cloned security servers located within the Cloud service provider's back-office infrastructure.

These services are the closest to commodity services that exist widely today. If you have identified others in your enterprise applications, then these should also be considered. Anything from claims services to remote PBX operations is possible today. JetBlue's live operators perform their jobs via telework.

Telework may also help operations in the event of a natural disaster or pandemic. A widely adopted telework strategy can also pay dividends in reduced commute times, reduced carbon footprint and increased worker satisfaction, which can reduce turnover. These intangibles are seldom discussed during times of relatively low fuel prices. Should the reverse be true, wouldn't it be handy to have the capabilities in case you need them, rather than to need them and not have them?

A typical telework application involves deploying a security appliance that allows connectivity to the internal IT network via a VPN connection. The typical VPN has a rating of the number of users that can connect. When this capacity is outstripped, a second box is added. The same sorts of issues apply to outsourcing the VPN connectivity: scalability, managing another piece of hardware and supporting the bandwidth required for coping with DoS attacks against the VPN box as well. This is another component that when pushed into the center of the Cloud may benefit from the bandwidth of the Cloud *versus* the bandwidth inside the enterprise.

Linking to expertise

Another benefit, as was mentioned earlier, is the concept of core competencies. If an activity only takes place infrequently, it is difficult to develop enough expertise to do it cost-effectively or well. By outsourcing these types of transaction to the Cloud, the amount of friction in the workforce can be reduced a little, and the overall quality can be increased.

Examples of what might fall into this category are not immediately apparent for an organization, but with the availability of numerous concierge and cottage services online, anything from law or financial advice to custom art on the fly is available through online services. This may be an accessible option for certain organizational services. As the Cloud evolves, the automation of selecting these services can also evolve along the same lines as online procurement for parts and components in the late 90s.

The same kinds of evolutionary shifts are/were promised in the services arena, where the best service, best mode of transport, tender offer and acceptance for contractual delivery occur without any human intervention. Subsequent efforts have not been proven to work completely to plan, but the framework is there and this may, in fact, represent one vision of the future of Cloud commerce.

Case study: backup and recovery centers

Using the Cloud simply to back up online and other corporate systems may be the easiest entry application yet. There are no particular requirements for speed other than that the data replication completes within a given period, and the data is accessible in the event of an emergency. Prior to this online replication, only specialized business continuity vendors provided what are known as hot sites.

Hot sites were prohibitively expensive, required tape transport and restoral time to get up and running. They were not dedicated facilities and could be oversubscribed, causing late declarers of disaster to be relocated to distant centers if the competition for facility space was overrun.

In a Cloud implementation, the remote Cloud is treated like a remote data vault and the vault is always available for deposits and withdrawals. In the event of an emergency, the data is accessed via the Internet; physical access is not required.

Case study: primary data centers

Next up the ladder is full-time data center consolidation: the Cloud as the data center. There can be more than one serving an organization. If one is disrupted, the others take over without missing a beat. This allows maximum flexibility.

If one data center is threatened by a hurricane, the other data centers take over processing. If another experiences a network outage, the others take up the slack. The ideal is 100% availability, 100% of the time. Since the average data recovery from tape can take hours, if not days, the redundancy can pay for itself many times over if it avoids even one such event.

Reducing the noise

One of the problems that make it difficult for chief information security officers (CISOs) to sleep at night is the number of smart machines in their network. With smart machines, you have the advantage of infinite configurability. This process dates back to the 80s and 90s when the Internet held nothing but promise and the operating system of the future would be the Internet.

In order to differentiate their products, browser manufacturers such as Netscape® and Microsoft® introduced plug-ins and add-ins that made Internet content more friendly, flashy and fun. This also introduced opportunities to configure these desktops on the fly via Internet content. It was only a matter of time before someone used these tools to deploy malicious code designed to alter, destroy or steal information via these same portals.

To get the noise down to a manageable level, you have two choices: either break things into very small pieces and combine similar traffic so anomalies stick out or have a machine look at all of the traffic and see if it can summarize and analyze enough traffic to find the bad stuff.

Attack surfaces multiply

Since centralized data centers are often much slower to deploy applications due to quality assurance and testing, many users woke up to the fact that with a PC, they could do a lot of their own development and analysis. This led to *ad hoc* additions of equipment and connections everywhere.

Now, every one of these *ad hoc* organizational assets is a vulnerability and a threat. If a field operator comes back to HQ and plugs in their laptop to check e-mail, they could unleash a firestorm of viruses and malware into the corporate network, once inside the walls. The firewalls are between you and the outside, so anything inside is fair game.

To make things worse, the typical network is pretty chatty. A copier/scanner/printer is sending out broadcasts to let everyone know it is online and has 50% magenta toner left, while the printer down the hall in engineering is out of paper. The firewall guarding the door keeps sending alerts back to corporate security that the sensor in room 208 is about to fail. All in all, a busy Manhattan street looks calm compared to the average departmental local area network (LAN).

This level of chatter makes it extremely difficult to catch any intruders. In point of fact, several studies indicate that malware is difficult to detect and until detected will persist on the network, allowing access, manipulation and extraction of data. This means that by the time a network breech is discovered, the perpetrators may have been on the network continuously for a long time. And they are fast learners. The most recent attacks have been geared towards finance and financial officers who may have access to online organizational banking accounts. Now, instead of several thousand dollars, a hacker may be able to grab millions.

These problems are exacerbated if the staff size is smaller. Smaller departments typically have only one full-time security person, if any at all. The same person may also be over the help desk. Move a department from one side of the office to the other and the last remaining ounce of security awareness could go with them.

Security in the Cloud

In the Fortune 1000, the typical network architecture routes traffic into a network operations center. The center is staffed 24/7/365 and looks for problems and reports from intrusion detection systems. Adopting this same strategy and moving your Internet connections into the monitored secure Cloud insures that the amount of traffic that is normally stopped at the corporate edge, clogging up the enterprise Internet pipe, will now be shed at the Cloud provider's pipe.

Only the filtered traffic will come through to the corporate network. This reduction in traffic will reduce the amount the corporate firewall has to deal with and will add a second layer of protection over the enterprise.

Monitoring hundreds of boxes for health, application health and security is indeed a gargantuan task. Managing this volume translates into managing risk. Security in the Cloud is performed by installing network monitors called sensors. These sensors look at all the traffic and report on any that looks suspicious.

There is a cafeteria approach with this type of service. Some functions may not be suitable to outsource; managing security appliances and reporting may be a commodity service, granting access to sensitive files may not be. Again, any action should be preceded by a full disclosure to stakeholders, a formal buy-in and continuous follow-up by the project leader on what is appropriate for the particular organization's culture.

Drop in additional protections such as intrusion detection software, network access protection and a 24/7 network operation center monitoring traffic and you start approaching the security from using a Cloud provider that would be available to a Fortune 1000 company with a full-time staff.

Server logs

With all of the hardware churning along, one of the ubiquitous trailing edges of all this technology is tracking compliance for security and adherence to organizational policy.

Most networked PCs, servers and firewalls produce their own internal security reports called logs. The typical report is a list of events with a date, time and description. For example, when a user mistypes their password, the system will list a failed sign-on attempt, the user id, the date and the time in the security log. A user who tries to enter a wrong password once may not be an issue. But a user that enters the wrong password ten times may be trying to break into the system.

Audit requirements and some industry regulations may require that these logs have to remain stored and accessible for a long period of time. Security analysis software will read the log, look for patterns and use reporting analytics to flag potential intrusion attempts and other dangerous symptoms such as failing or overheated hardware.

Following these logs is a full-time job in itself. Increasing the number of servers also multiplies the volume of server logs. Companies such as ArcSight have made a business out of reading all of the logs and storing them offline.

Since they take up a lot of network storage space, some vendors are now specializing in storing these logs in the Cloud and producing alerts if the Cloud service provider notices a potential problem. This can be a valuable service for SMBs that may not have the staff available to monitor these systems.

Coupling these with intrusion detection capabilities provides a second set of eyes to watch your network. With statistics heavily in favor of when your network is penetrated *versus* if, it may be prudent to invest in any and all of these technologies.

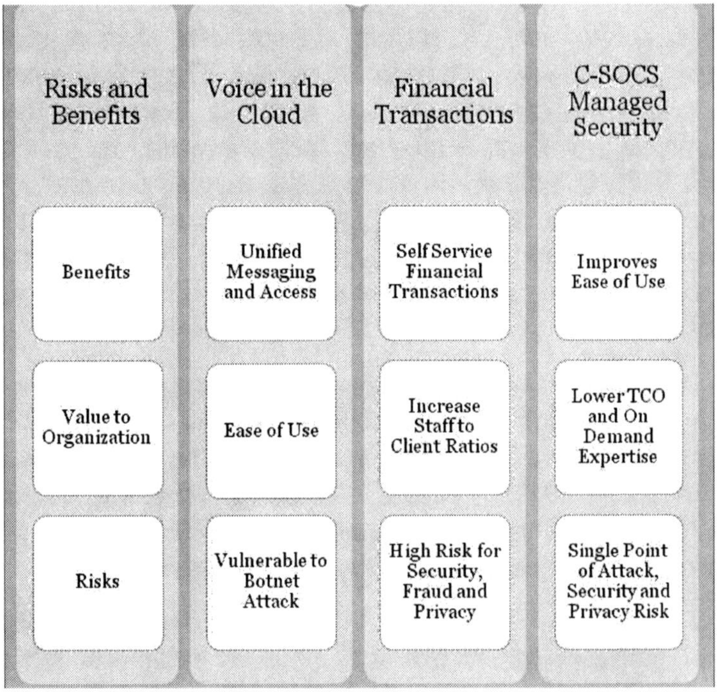

Risks and Benefits	Voice in the Cloud	Financial Transactions	C-SOCS Managed Security
Benefits	Unified Messaging and Access	Self Service Financial Transactions	Improves Ease of Use
Value to Organization	Ease of Use	Increase Staff to Client Ratios	Lower TCO and On Demand Expertise
Risks	Vulnerable to Botnet Attack	High Risk for Security, Fraud and Privacy	Single Point of Attack, Security and Privacy Risk

Figure 14: Cloud caution apps

Linking systems dynamically

Once we have developed more than one Cloud, it will be natural to want to connect some of these via the Internet. Already the processes and protocols are in place. What may be missing is the logic or programming. If I have a geographic database of roads and streets, how much better could it be if I can add a layer of surveillance cameras and local temperature sensors?

Once I have these layers, can I also go further and dispatch snow and ice trucks based on average thermal coverage? What if several cities own the surveillance and sensors, yet I am responsible for truck dispatch and overall view?

These types of issues can be solved but require a greater degree of interoperability and cooperation. The overall end result looks attractive and it may be possible to broker access to the consolidated product to those who work well with the consolidation. The good news is that this type of consolidation is technically possible.

Mashups

The Cloud may represent a virtual storefront of data feeds and data products, combined via mashup, open source tinkering and wiki magic to form patterns of data where before there were only raw feeds.

The open source people refer to these as metadata repositories. The description is data about data. By creating automated tools that can read the data about data and then pursue some logical action on the metadata, more complex relationships can be formed on the fly.

An example might be to tie the yellow pages with data like addresses and types of business to a geographic information system, which is basically a map with metadata tags like address, lat–long points, city, state, and county and zip information. This is the sort of mashup that might lead a global positioning system (GPS) plot point on the geographic information system (GIS) system to query where the closest Thai restaurants are close to zip 22042.

Once you can envision the mapping layer, now imagine real-time feeds from the sources for information like the current prices of gasoline by grade. From this, a smart in-vehicle telematics device can now answer questions like what the closest and cheapest petrol stations are within a mile.

This is not a Cloud activity in particular, but it may take a globally accessible data repository to take full advantage of the merger of metadata, localized inputs and smart telemetry to drive local behavior. Key to the success of these collaborations is following standard formats for data streams. Use of XML and protocols such as Google™ Maps and Google™ Transit will help accelerate this trend.

Privacy *versus* security

The dark side is that when there is total awareness, there is a total lack of privacy. Add another layer of GPS tracking information from bank cards, in-vehicle telematics and GPS-enabled smartphones and there is very little left to the imagination.

The ability to check a Blackberry® into a hotel safe so that the guest can have a break from constant accessibility is only one sign that we may be approaching a tipping point in this regard. The bank debit card has already been posited for several years as one of the best ways to track someone. Add in a bit of organized external GPS awareness of mobile devices and there may be some justification for concern.

In asking a question, these devices can also possibly inadvertently reveal the location of the device. The issue of privacy concerns regarding telematics is in its infancy. If a malicious actor could tap into telematic GPS reporting, they might use the GPS for malicious purposes such as cyberstalking.

A few years ago, a plumber fraudulently requested the installation of remote call forwarding on a phone number belonging to a busy competitor. When his own business was slow, he would simply forward his competitor's phone to his phone until he received a call. Once he got the competitor's business, he would un-forward the phone. In this way, it is estimated he deprived the competing plumber of US$300,000 worth of business.

Now, this particular service requires significant proof of identity before the telecom company will allow it to be installed. We should consider that similar controls will need to be implemented to protect GPS-enabled mobile devices in order to prevent a malicious actor from tracking another user's GPS device.

Organizing the Cloud environment

Balancing privacy concerns *versus* shared services is the essence of the Cloud's environment stresses on corporate security and privacy advocates. On the one hand, there is not much difference between a physical device and a virtualized image of the same.

The lack of management tools, the relatively young age of these types of system and the overall and increasing complexity of today's computing environment makes for a complex stew of concerns, so it is no wonder that there is not a consensus for how to do this kind of implementation, much less to answer the question as to why.

The portal model

The portal model is a relatively easy methodology to organize access and information. A true portal has one sign-on. From this sign-on, all information one is authorized to view is accessible. This matches in simplicity the old user menus available on iSeries® and mainframe CICS® systems. Sign on, and you see a menu of choices. Some are menus of menus of choices. Regardless, by selecting one item you can add, update or change something, view something or perhaps ask the system to calculate and print reports about something.

The Cloud environment can work the same way. Your organization may not have converted all information over to the Cloud. Also, since some Cloud applications will not work with others, there may be limited convergence of multiple Cloud systems.

So going back to some familiar examples, let's look at something like a customer relationship management (CRM) package and e-mail. Both feature information such as who, what, and how much business may be solely in the CRM database. The e-mail for each customer would normally be in there as well.

Ask for an e-mail to be sent to each customer with over US$50,000 in business and the integration is complete. The e-mail server can now be populated with all customers with business over US$50,000. Select the e-mail application, edit the e-mail and away they go.

The portal is a convenient notional way to envision the Cloud. Sign on to the portal and you can access information that is pertinent only to you. Sign off and the information is hidden. Bring on a new application and the next time you sign on, your portal reveals it to you. Sign off and it is gone.

If you are a Cloud service provider, what is critical for you to attract and retain loyal clientele?

- Integrity – both in business practices and in absolute care in executing transactions.
- Discretion – privacy must be maintained within the spirit and letter of the law where the organization is conducting business.
- Security – applies to origination, transport, storage and access to information that resides in and transverses the Cloud environment.
- Equality – all customers must be treated with respect and the same bill of rights applies no matter how big or how small.
- Scalability – the clients are seeking out Cloud Computing for scalability. This means that excess capacity must be built into the Cloud environment. The good news is that since this a shared resource, it is likely that the efficiency of the Cloud environment will be greater than the sum of its parts if they were deployed individually.

This last point has been made many times before as a justification for Cloud Computing. The cost benefits and increased utilization make up for the loss of control, increased transport costs and risk of disclosure (assuming the Cloud-hosting organization is a third party and not a captive entity.)

If you are a user of Cloud services, what is your perspective?

- Price – must meet or exceed internal costs for the same service.

- Performance – must meet or exceed internal performance measures. (You do have internal performance measures?)

- Service levels – this may be the most difficult area to agree upon. What services will the Cloud provider provide? Do they include patching and maintenance? How often? How secure? How will you know?

If you are a third-party auditor, what is your perspective?

- Prove the service levels are in alignment with agreed standards – testing transaction turnarounds and various network-centric controls are in place.

- Prove the security is adequate – the HR controls on employee pre-screening and post-hire training are auditable. (Most larger organizations use LMSs.) An LMS system maintains a list of courses, provides online training and testing, maintains a record of the curriculum required, and whether the staff member or contractor has completed the required training. Lack of training, and security awareness training in particular, is a red flag for lack of concern by top management. This usually means multiple other security protocols are given lax treatment as well.

- Prove the continuity plan is in place, tested and will work upon demand – check the existence of documentation that there is a plan and review the plan to determine if it has ever been successfully tested. From a Cloud perspective, data replication is pretty much assumed. But don't take this for granted. Some Cloud environments are so large and daunting that no one has ever bothered to test whether the controls are in place.

During one incident, in the fall of 2008, a Cloud hosting provider lost 100,000 websites over one weekend due to hacking activity. Initial analysis led to the conclusion that the hacking was made possible by not changing default passwords on some of the database engines.

The lesson here is that the size of the organization (100,000 website-hosting company) is not necessarily indicative that the organization is following the best practices, or that it even has a clue what those practices are.

A similar event occurred with the Microsoft® subsidiary Danger that hosted the Sidekick phone database. All users' contacts and information stored in the Cloud disappeared overnight with "little hope of getting it back". Eventually they were able to get most of it back, but it's still a warning to those on the same road.

Pilot projects

The good thing about pilots is that they can reveal cultural and procedural hurdles that may be taken into account in negotiation and/or killing deals before they go too far.

The bad thing about pilots is that they may be too small to test scalability. Trying to match scale with a Cloud test may exceed anyone's resources. The good news is that a Cloud vendor of some heft should be able to demonstrate substantial excess capacity.

They should also be able to articulate how often the Cloud is replicated and to where (what country or continent?). If the Cloud data or backup is accessible by any staff, under what circumstances can they access data, and what vendors have access to the data? If vendors have access, they should also articulate how they vet staff, as well.

Backing up the Cloud

Building in resiliency

From the business impact analysis (BIA) to the business continuity strategy, there is a lot of leeway. The main issue with Cloud Computing is that it promises resiliency. This resiliency does not come without a price and it does not come automatically. Understanding what has to be done is tied to understanding what is a) critical, and b) required to restore these critical systems in an emergency.

Data recovery testing

Restoring a file on the fly, or even restoring in any case, is a daunting task. Being sure you need to restore the file is a great first step. The files represent freedom for the end-user, responsibility for the monitors. It is difficult even for an expert to tell someone else it's time to back up, we may not be able to save this, etc.

Try you must, in any case. The difficulty lies in starting, not necessarily the details of the actual successful case. These cases depend on a) the treatment of mystery elements, and b) a steady stream of recruits.

Business continuity testing

Once the basic plan is in place, it is important to test it. Testing takes the initial form of a tabletop exercise. Bring the stakeholders together and walk through the plan. If it works, documentation is complete. If it doesn't (far more likely for first efforts) then it needs to be adjusted accordingly.

What value is added by the Cloud?

There is a common approach in internal IT departments which is as follows:

- The organization identifies a problem or need.
- The organization directs management to find a solution.
- A solution is proposed and accepted by the organization.
- IT develops and implements the solution.

Once the program is completed, control is passed over to operational units. The required steps to maintain continuity of the operational system are taken and the system enters the normal life cycle of use, modification and replacement.

The core issue with major programs that follow this path is that the organization may not have all of the players trained, knowledgeable and ready to make this transition. In the case of a complex system such as ERP or even in the case of a Microsoft® Exchange or SharePoint® upgrade, the steps required may only be executed once a year or even once every five years.

The core competencies of the IT staff are only a degree or two apart from the operational system. Unless rigorous effort is undertaken to train them and keep them trained, they may not have the required technical skills. This leads to implementation missteps, blown deadlines and, in extreme cases, blown unrecoverable systems.

If you take into account that complex systems such as SAP®, Oracle® or PeopleSoft® can have tens of thousands of individual settings, any one of which may have a major impact on the behavior of the production system, this complexity lends itself to problems that may be unpredictable and outside the control of the program manager.

This is all well and good if the organization has the resources to test the transition using a full production test with similar workloads. The average bottom line or budget may not support this in SMBs. The result is that any major system change can potentially be life threatening to the organization.

Complexity equals inherent risk

Cloud Computing, SaaS, IaaS and PaaS will not sidestep all of these change management risks. Indeed, they can amplify them if care is not taken in the transition.

From a project management perspective, these types of concerns should be brought out on the front end of any consideration to adopt a new process. An organization's adoption of project management best practices and process improvement strategies to build in stakeholder buy-in, and project scope and charter will enable the organization to make better decisions, structure projects with more realistic reach, and improve the chance of success.

From the standpoint of highly complex, customized applications with idiosyncratic development concepts, these may be last on the list to convert to the Cloud. If, on the other hand, you have generic commodity processes such as e-mail, wikis, blogs and social networking applications, it may be worth considering moving these to the top.

For the most part, these comparisons fall into the make-or-buy decisions already in the institutional DNA for any outsourced services. There are not many degrees of separation from Cloud Computing to the outsourcing contracts of the 80s and 90s. Just because the vendor is "Cloud based," it doesn't mean that it has people, processes and technologies that can't fail. It hopefully means that the people, processes and technologies are more robust than those that the organization might adopt on its own.

Reduce the complexity of the organization

The main path through this is:

1 Look at the risks;
2 Determine how to reduce the risks.
3 Plan for the worst.
4 Test what would happen and how to react if you experience the worst.
5 Make sure you know who your cyber doppelgangers are and how to get in touch with them, wherever they may be.

Start over; try it again.

Major efforts to duplicate this course over multiple agencies and multiple sites may be a bit daunting for larger organizations. The main things to bear in mind are:

• You don't have to do it all at once.
• Start somewhere small and manageable.
• Make sure this is an early success instead of an overreaching failure.

To do this may require dialing down the initial effort to one application on one server somewhere. Once this one is in the bag and working successfully, a larger undertaking can be tried.

It is important to consider that the internal organization does not operate in a vacuum. It has processes and procedures in place (hopefully) to recover from any major disruption. Consideration should be made early on for the possible impact that removing some of these operations from internal recovery procedures might have on the overall recovery. Hopefully, an internal disruption will be able to avoid contamination of the externally outsourced operations. The disrupted external operations will be able to quickly recover from any one disruption.

As might be expected, there are probably easy-to-use applications that would not present a great deal of risk to adopt within the Cloud, such as training applications like maintenance manuals and LMSs.

E-mail service and web hosting

Starting in the mid 80s, malicious actors started using tools to attack networks. On a personal level, this was called flaming, sending so much traffic at an individual user that they could no longer stay online.

These types of attacks are called DoS attacks. Using multiple machines to launch this type of attack is called a DDoS attack (pronounced dee-dos). Hackers now use armies of infected machines called bots, organized into "herds" called "botnets" to launch these attacks on sites in attempts to extort money or simply to put them out of service to make a political or personal statement.

The best defenses against these attacks currently have more bandwidth than the attacker or install high-performance network firewalls that can recognize that an attack is taking place and drop the offending packets before they can flood the network and slow it down.

By pushing websites and e-mail services into the Cloud, an organization may be able to sidestep some of these sorts of attack by partnering with a Cloud-based Internet service provider with these types of defense in place.

Cloud-based enterprise applications

The more complex endeavors such as ERP and CRM software may present additional opportunities, given the complexity of installation in-house, for the adoption of a Cloud model that features Cloud-based expert support and Cloud provisioning that can surge to support enterprise-sized workloads without worrying about the infrastructure, architects and software experts for the particular platform.

Using Web 2.0 to support internal clients

The Web 2.0 forces of change may put pressure on traditional business units to convert to keep up. The Cloud paradigm has similar notional pressures. However, the lather, rinse, repeat cycle of agile programming techniques and Web 2.0 mashups have some uses in traditional models. One such use might even be to set up a web blog within the organization to determine what the risks and rewards might be for Cloud adoption.

The common complaint about ivory-towered IT is that it is unresponsive. There are many reasons for this; however, the main issue could be that the noise and strife associated with maintaining existing systems has cut off all but a few IT staff from actually communicating with the end-users. If the situation is to be remedied, a wiki or blog segregated by communities of users might be helpful.

Frameworks for process improvement

This can start off with a common complaints page on the organization's intranet.

- Did you know you can reset your own password? Here is the link.
- Did you know that removing and reseating the battery of your smartphone can fix many problems with your phone?
- Did you know that entering your issue via our web link will actually help us solve your problem 10 times faster? Here's how.

Allowing for feedback on this type of forum may result in some negative postings. However, it is much better to have the negative feedback so that your organization can address it, than not have it and think all is well.

Case study: voice in the Clouds

About the time that Vonage and SmartJack got firmly entrenched in TV advertising, there was probably a similar earthquake in corporate communications and especially corporate PBX manufacturers. The same drivers from landlines to cell phones are affecting their corporate cousins. Adoption of an Internet-based phone system with integrated voice messaging and e-mail messaging seems to be quite attractive.

6: Take Off

If we can move my e-mail to the Cloud, can we move my voicemail along with it? Depending on what your organization does for a living, the impact of voice availability may not be high on the scale or it may be the only thing that keeps business rolling in. The same sorts of risk assessment apply in telecoms. The bright side is that Internet-based voice has a low cost of entry; it lends itself to outsourcing; it requires massive amounts of bandwidth to support at the core, but maybe not so much at the edge.

An Internet voice provider can be just as prone to attack as an Internet web provider. There are malwares floating around the labs that are designed to hijack and echo voice calls made on the Internet to tap, as it were, the phone calls passing through cyberspace. The landline equivalent, on the other hand, has built-in safeguards such as carrier-based security controls over voice traffic, and last-mile physical security controls.

The only reasonable way to tap a phone call is at the edge in the handset, or in the building or central phone office at the wiring closet. Getting into the central office requires recruiting a willing accomplice or inserting a willing accomplice through the hiring process. All possible, but a bit more difficult to accomplish in practice.

Voice over IP (VoIP) calls can be tapped if the VoIP system or one of the client devices is penetrated, so there is some risk. This remains an attractive Cloud service simply because of the potential to reduce cost and integrate services such as voicemail and e-mail messaging into one mailbox.

The downsides are: VoIP is a real-time protocol; it is also susceptible to DDoS attacks and other Internet disruptions. If your organization revolves around voice, consider the risks of a major disruption and implement hybrid approaches that allow for failover to solid landline circuits or use landline as the primary and allow VoIP to serve as surge and failover for the landlines in place.

Quality of service and net neutrality

Other issues that are peripheral to this are the subject of net neutrality. Net neutrality states that all traffic is equal on the Internet. Therefore voice calls (even though in real time) are equal to e-mail packets and even malware packets. Therefore, prioritization of the voice packets for any other type of traffic is forbidden under net neutrality rules. This may not play out in practice, with some services allowing for quality of service rules to take effect within their own network's span of control, but once the traffic is handed off to another provider (as is usually the case), the net neutrality rules kick back in and the packets are back to best effort to reach the remote session's system.

If you rely on voice for reservations or customer service, plan for the worst case and take advantage of the price performance where possible.

JetBlue did this, with all reservations agents working from home with flexible schedules and a broadband connection. Since the agents were distributed across the country, a single agent could lose their connection, but all agents simultaneously would be unlikely to do so. The benefit to JetBlue was that less room was required to set up initial operations, in addition to happier, more productive users.

Another transportation company turned all of the claims processing into telework positions, since the calls were random and could be processed online using their image-enabled technology. They saved floor space in their expanding business and reduced the pressure on capital expenditure to expand the headquarters.

Dozens of other transportation companies have used Cloud services to outsource their logs and paperwork scanning to the Cloud. By outsourcing the labor-intensive paperwork scanning to truck stops, they were able to reduce centralized staff and floor-space requirements, reduce overnight shipping costs and cut the time required to process billing by nearly three days. In terms of financing costs, multiply the daily cost of money by the total accounts receivable (A/R) outstanding and you are close to the direct cost reduction possible through this type of process improvement.

These are just a few examples of the opportunities available through pursuing a web-centric/Cloud strategy and more are no doubt available by thinking through your existing organizational constraints.

Case study: online storage in the Cloud

One of the low-hanging fruits for Cloud environments is Cloud bursting. Cloud bursting refers to reaching out to preconfigured data-storage Clouds to store information on either a temporary or permanent basis. This can be used for data backup and disaster recovery or as a precursor to more sophisticated services such as external storage of system logs and security analysis.

Using the Cloud for disaster recovery consists of providing a duplicate hardware and software environment that the organization can use as a hot site. By installing replication software, the data can be fed back to the host Cloud continuously.

If the primary system is unavailable, the users can switch to the Cloud. Care must be taken when switching back since the Cloud system will have transactions that weren't on the primary. A backup or catch-up routine of some sort must be run in order to recover the new transactions from the Cloud.

This can help sort out document sharing, reduce duplication of storage elsewhere and bring together communities of interest. It is also making significant information readily accessible via the Internet.

Data loss prevention

These types of control fit into the generic security software practice known as data loss prevention. The software capabilities that can resolve this issue are available in somewhat nascent form and there may be ongoing issues as to their effectiveness. Again, returning to the conservative argument, what is the worst that could happen if this information was released or viewed inappropriately? If the answer is not good, not good at all, then you may need to consider higher levels of controls before proceeding. If these controls exceed the cost of conversion, then private Clouds certainly will be in your future along with public Clouds.

This type of implementation, where some data is transparent and accessible via the Cloud and some is hidden away inside the organizational private Cloud, is termed a hybrid Cloud. There is not likely to be one answer that will fit all organizations, but the Cloud Computing matrix is sufficiently flexible to adjust to meet most needs.

Case study: moving a webzine to the Cloud

Jill has decided to modernize and re-architect a youth-oriented webzine (redesign the plumbing that makes the website run). The webzine was launched on a corporate web server, doesn't actually sell anything, but does bring in a bit of advertising revenue and sells other products for the company.

Since the number of hits started increasing, the rest of the corporate web traffic is starting to experience performance problems, and in one case an attack on the teen site brought down the rest of the corporate traffic.

Using her classical IT education, Jill knows that moving anything for any reason requires a continuity of operations plan. Starting from square one, she determines the following scenarios.

Assessing the risk

1   Do nothing. The site will continue to degrade performance. If no infrastructure is upgraded, the corporate traffic will degrade along with the webzine traffic increases and increased attacks. The webzine is at risk as well if performance drives down the number of hits, and click-through advertising revenue will drop as well.
2   Install dedicated circuit for the webzine. This will increase capital and operational expenses. Since this is a start-up, there is an increased risk that finance will kill the project before it has a chance to gain traction and catch on. Viral marketing techniques and word of mouth have been adding traffic monthly, but without the infrastructure upgrade, the traffic continues to drive negative values.
3   Migrate to a Web 2.0 Cloud web host. This will allow access to an operational expense model. As the web traffic grows, the number of web servers can be automatically increased. Since there are no links to corporate backend databases, the move should be relatively straightforward. The actual links to purchase products are already forwarded to other payment processing sites in the Cloud. The main issue with moving is selecting a partner that is strong enough financially to maintain operations over the growth period of the webzine and at the same time maintain adequate security controls to reduce the risk of host-caused disruption.

Organizational impact assessment

If the webzine continues to grow, doing nothing will result in having to make a Solomon's choice, the corporate traffic *versus* the webzine traffic. In the worst case scenario, the webzine can be brought down and the site will appear unreachable to the external networks. This will result in the tarnishing of the webzine brand, but the corporate traffic can continue unimpeded.

If Jill adds a dedicated circuit and more web hardware, she will be able to insulate the rest of the organization's networks from attacks against the webzine. The costs will increase modestly with the additional circuit. If the webzine fails to gain a foothold, the enterprise may wind up eating some costs on the extra bandwidth in terms of web-server hardware and installation costs, plus a commitment of keeping the additional circuit for at least a year. The bandwidth and hardware could be repurposed, but are not necessary otherwise.

If Jill selects a Cloud or managed service option, she will not require any additional hardware and will not increase her capital expenditure. The cost of renting a website is relatively light and can be paid for month to month. The existing hardware used for the webzine can be repurposed or retired. Since it is a sunk cost, this alternative does not add any costs to the capital expense budget. This alternative is less expensive than option 2 and does not have the same level of risk of tarnishing the brand as option 1. Lower risk, more fulfilling!

Continuity plans

Jill determines that if there is a hardware failure or an extended attack on the site, it may be down for up to three days. Since the environment is very competitive, a three-day outage is unacceptable from a business standpoint. She would prefer an uninterruptible site so she can compete head to head with the established teen webzines.

She adds the following to a request for proposal:

- Provide web hosting for up to 1,000,000 simultaneous visitors for the teen webzine.
- Provide enough bandwidth to survive a DDoS attack (10GB per second minimum).
- Provide at least two physical sites in case the main hosting site is down. (Note: just because it is in the Cloud, it doesn't

mean there aren't servers in a server room somewhere. If you don't ask, it is possible the hosting provider will only maintain one site.)

- Maintain a service level agreement (SLA) for a 1 second response time through 1,000,000 simultaneous users.
- Charge based on a sliding scale based on website traffic.

Jill receives several responses. To narrow down the field, she discards all responses that have not answered all of her requests. Because there are some additional concerns raised by IT on the quality of the responses, Jill engages an outside firm to provide neutral third-party assessments of the bidders' responses. The third-party firm adds some security and HR questions to a request for information (RFI). The short-listed firms respond to the RFI and the third party recommends that two be dropped for lack of an internal training program, and that a third be dropped for lack of HR background checks on the staff-hiring process.

Of the remaining four:

- Company 1 has been in business just over a year and specializes in cheap, fast hosting.

- Company 2 has been in business five years and has provided a SAS 70 report by a private accounting firm featuring a summary of their operational controls.

- Company 3 has been in business seven years and has provided tier IV fault tolerance certification, indicating a high level of redundancy in the data center. They also indicated they have a second data center at tier III level of redundancy.

- Company 4 has also been in business five years and has provided ISO27001 certification.

Since company 3 is the least expensive and also has a backup site in order to qualify for tier IV, Jill is leaning towards selecting them. The consultant, however, offers the following response:

- Company 1 doesn't have the track record to determine their reliability. They are the cheapest but not necessarily the lowest risk. If this was an internal social networking site, the consultant offered, they might be worth using simply to keep costs down.

- Company 2 has a SAS 70 report. Since this is provided by a company that is beholden to the firm for repeat business, the SAS 70 may not go into enough detail or be aggressive enough to ferret out problems. The SAS 70 in and of itself would not be enough to select this one over the others. In addition, the company may not release the detailed SAS 70 report. They may just disclose that they have one. Additional questions and perhaps a site visit would be necessary to really assess their level of competence.

- Company 3 has taken a higher level of care to get the tier IV certification. The tier IV does not guarantee a backup site, merely that all facilities have backups at the same site. They do have a second data center with similar redundancy so would probably represent a relative improvement over the status quo.

- Company 4 has gone above and beyond. In order to qualify for ISO27001 certification, the company must submit to a rigorous certification of not only the infrastructure, but also the processes and the verifiable adherence to the processes by the staff. This is the extra edge that the consultant was looking for. In terms of selection, the consultant does not have a favorite, but indicates to Jill that out of the four companies, 3 and 4 should definitely be worth considering since 3 has sought independent verifiable certification of fault tolerance and 4 has sought independent verifiable certification of process.

Jill asks some more questions and opts for Company 4 upon receiving their assurances on the provision of fault tolerance as well. She sets up a project plan that effectively leaves the existing site up while the new Cloud-based site is tested. Following additional recommendations by the consultant, Jill has the new site tested for security vulnerabilities as well.

Since the webzine site is on the Internet, any security vulnerability may allow a hacker to alter the site or post links that lead to other bad sites. Jill works with the hosting company to set up a continuous scan of the web content for security vulnerabilities.

She has also implemented Web 2.0 blogs and comments. Along with the normal system logs, the blogs and comments are also scanned by the hosting company for inappropriate content.

She also instructs the company to add buttons so a webzine user can flag content as like, don't like or block it. That way, if users discover a problem, they will have an easy way to report bad content or abuse to help her maintain her brand and feel even more attached to the webzine community. Block votes would be forwarded to Jill for further action if necessary.

Now that the hosting company has been selected, and the site has been tested, the process of launching the new site is scheduled. The launch date selected is a Wednesday, based on the lightest traffic load, and the availability of technical staff.

On the Monday before, a link is added to the old site announcing the availability of the beta site. The URL for the beta site is slightly different than the host site. At the time of the launch, the new URL and the old URL are requested to point to the same data center.

As this change propagates through the Internet domain-name servers, more and more traffic starts to show up on the new site and the traffic on the old site starts to drop. Eventually, the old site traffic drops to near zero.

Jill instructs the IT staff to put in a HTML redirect page in case there are some stragglers that are pointing to the old site. Within a short time, the traffic does go to zero and the old server is retired.

This is provided as an illustration of the continuity model for planning. The risk assessment, the gap analysis and the continuity planning are critical steps to avoid missteps in moving into the Cloud environment for the first time.

This case study is representative of the sort of planning required to implement a standalone product such as a web community page or an e-mail service.

CHAPTER 7: ABOVE THE CLOUDS

An understanding of the current environment, the risks and rewards of converting, the number of hurdles, and internal stakeholder support all have to be factored into making any conversion project successful.

Starting along this path is never easy. It is critical to consider what will be gained from a successful implementation. It is also critical to consider what might be lost if the implementation fails.

Transition

Determine what is crucial in your current environment, what key applications are contributing to your success, and which applications are or are not commodities.

Start a dialogue internally regarding which applications the current users think are important. If an application works well, is only used by a few dozen and doesn't need to be updated, it may not be a good candidate for Cloud conversion.

If, on the other hand, an application is constantly breaking, has back-level or nonexistent vendor software support and the hardware may not be available as a hot site or on the used market, the organization may already be at significant risk simply by staying put. The cost of doing nothing may be much greater if the current system has no reasonable recovery path.

Convergence

The adoption of Cloud Computing at an individual, small business or large organization level will take very different pathways. The main advantage is that the large scale of the hosting platforms enables all adoptees to share in the benefits of the Cloud environment.

Technologies that once were only in reach of the few are now accessible to all. Driving the convergence to a Cloud environment must be the people and the process. The technology is always secondary.

The Cloud is still a solution but it is not the only solution. As Wal-Mart did in the 80s, disconnecting the software from the platform produces an opportunity to select from a plethora of vendors. By decoupling the people and process from the technology, we can do the same.

The simplification of the computing environment requires more sophistication of the apps in the Cloud. The proliferation of smartphones such as the Blackberry® and the iPhone™ may point the way to the next generation of computing: always on, stable, proprietary platforms, limited functionality, but with limited attack surface and vulnerability.

The paradigm of the automated teller machine

When the first automated teller machines (ATMs) appeared, they quickly went from one in every city to one on every street corner. The success of the ATM is due in part to the simplicity of the interface. No keyboard except for numeric, and choices limited by menu to a few options. Once you understand how it works, you don't have to be retrained.

The same sorts of functionality can exist in the Cloud with applications becoming more sophisticated, yet easier for users, as simplicity gains traction in the workplace.

Trading functionality for security

In order to make this simplicity work in practice, the user has to accept the limitations of the device. Taking this analogy to the Cloud, the same limited-functionality devices are starting to appear. The HP Dreamscreen is geared towards home use, provides ubiquitous computing with a touch screen and the only apps are in the Cloud.

The Amazon Kindle™ and Sony readers are similar with simple, single-function devices that work and don't bring along a wave of vulnerabilities behind them.

This lowers the bar for adoption. It may represent a good strategy to catch technology up within the organization and presage an eventual outsourcing down the road as IT commodity services are formally identified.

Staged conversion: parallel testing

Assuming that more applications are moved to the Cloud, the result for internal staff could be a force multiplier. By not having to support commodity operations, they can now concentrate on core business systems and concerns. Outsource the trivial or commodities-based, and then concentrate on what will differentiate your business.

This will free up staff, lower operational costs, lower capital expense and introduce scalability. No longer will you have to wait while server C is upgraded to handle additional users, or migrate accounts off one server to another to support staff growth.

The capabilities and amount of information available on the Internet dwarf the amount available only a year ago. As the Clouds continue to evolve, we will find new ways to join Clouds together, stepping from one to the other seamlessly.

If we need a map, if we need a translation, if we need an analysis or process, there will be a Cloud with the information floating separate and apart above a sea of processing. From below, the Clouds will still seem dark and impenetrable. However, from our perch high above, the Clouds reflect nothing but light.

ITG RESOURCES

IT Governance Ltd. sources, creates and delivers products and services to meet the real-world, evolving IT governance needs of today's organisations, directors, managers and practitioners. The ITG website (*www.itgovernance.co.uk*) is the international one-stop-shop for corporate and IT governance information, advice, guidance, books, tools, training and consultancy. *www.itgovernance.co.uk/cloud-computing.aspx* is the information page from our website which shows our Cloud Computing resources.

Other Websites

Books and tools published by IT Governance Publishing (ITGP) are available from all business booksellers and are also immediately available from the following websites:

www.itgovernance.co.uk/catalog/355 provides information and online purchasing facilities for every currently available book published by ITGP.

www.itgovernanceusa.com is a US$-based website that delivers the full range of IT Governance products to North America, and ships from within the continental US.

www.itgovernanceasia.com provides a selected range of ITGP products specifically for customers in South Asia.

www.27001.com is the IT Governance Ltd. website that deals specifically with information security management, and ships from within the continental US.

Pocket Guides

For full details of the entire range of pocket guides, simply follow the links at *www.itgovernance.co.uk/publishing.aspx*.

Toolkits

ITG's unique range of toolkits includes the IT Governance Framework Toolkit, which contains all the tools and guidance that you will need in order to develop and implement an appropriate IT governance framework for your organisation. Full details can be found at *www.itgovernance.co.uk/ products/519*.

For a free paper on how to use the proprietary CALDER-MOIR IT Governance Framework, and for a free trial version of the toolkit, see *www.itgovernance.co.uk/calder_moir.aspx*.

There is also a wide range of toolkits to simplify implementation of management systems, such as an ISO/IEC 27001 ISMS or a BS25999 BCMS, and these can all be viewed and purchased online at: *http://www.itgovernance.co.uk/catalog/1*

Best Practice Reports

ITG's range of Best Practice Reports is now at *www.itgovernance.co.uk/best-practice-reports.aspx*. These offer you essential, pertinent, expertly researched information on an increasing number of key issues including Web 2.0 and Green IT.

Training and Consultancy

IT Governance also offers training and consultancy services across the entire spectrum of disciplines in the information governance arena. Details of training courses can be accessed at *www.itgovernance.co.uk/training.aspx* and descriptions of our consultancy services can be found at *http://www.itgovernance.co.uk/consulting.aspx*.
Why not contact us to see how we could help you and your organisation?

Newsletter

IT governance is one of the hottest topics in business today, not least because it is also the fastest moving, so what better way to keep up than by subscribing to ITG's free monthly newsletter *Sentinel*? It provides monthly updates and resources across the whole spectrum of IT governance subject matter, including risk management, information security, ITIL and IT service management, project governance, compliance and so much more. Subscribe for your free copy at: *www.itgovernance.co.uk/newsletter.aspx*.

CPSIA information can be obtained at www.ICGtesting.com
Printed in the USA
BVOW020454030212

282009BV00006B/19/P